A SAFE PLACE TO LAND

A Journey

Through

Unexpected Loss

and Recovery

E. J. HUTCHISON

ISBN: 978-1-970730-92-0

Published by

Fideli Publishing, Inc.
119 W. Morgan St.
Martinsville, IN 46151
www.FideliPublishing.com

DEDICATION

I dedicate this book to my Lord and Savior, Jesus Christ, who has given me the opportunity to be transparent for those who have suffered, lost, and hurt, and for those who thought there was no way past the pain they didn't see coming. May this book help restore, rebuild, and renew all that God has for you.

TABLE OF CONTENTS

Restoration falls on all those who are married.
We need to put in perspective the true meaning
of what it means to be a husband and a wife.
In doing so, it gives us an accountability first to God,
because He created marriage, and second to man,
because the world is constantly looking for the meaning
and example of what true marriage looks and sounds like.

— E. J. Hutchison

FOREWORD

This is not a book you simply read — it's one you experience. From the first page, the author speaks with raw honesty about identity, manhood, faith, and healing. His story begins with success that feels hollow and a whisper from God saying, there's more. What follows is a spiritual journey of surrender — shedding ego, redefining strength, and learning that real manhood isn't found in performance, but in submission to God. His writing invites readers to remove the mask of survival and trust the process of becoming whole.

At its core, this book reclaims what it means to walk in purpose and relationship — with God, with self, and with others. Through his "Brother to Brother" and "Brother to Sister" reflections, the author speaks truth to both men and women — challenging men to grow beyond fear disguised as swagger and calling women to pray over men's becoming, not control it. Every page reminds us that the wilderness is not punishment, but preparation; not the end, but the birthplace of transformation.

The love story threaded through these chapters reflects divine timing and reverent obedience. It's not about passion alone, but purpose — love rooted in faith, discipline, and mutual surrender. Through temptation, loss, rediscovery, and restraint, we see that when God authors a story, He also sets the pace. The devotional sections and reflection questions turn the book into a personal guide for anyone ready to replace striving with surrender and image with intimacy.

This book is a gift to both the broken and the brave. It offers language for pain, permission to

heal, and a roadmap for spiritual maturity. The author doesn't present perfection — he presents process. And in doing so, he shows us that grace is not just what meets us after failure — it's what walks with us through becoming.

— Dr. Marie Brown-Mercadel
Certified Trauma Coach, TEDx Speaker,
Author of *Getting to My Enough* and
The Intersection Between Faith and Forgiveness

AUTHOR'S NOTE

Thank you for being here. This book is titled *A Safe Place to Land* because every person deserves a space where they can breathe, reflect, and rebuild. Life brings challenges, and none of us escape pain. Hurt happens. Loss happens. Change happens. What defines us is not the struggle itself, but the way we move through it and the grace we allow ourselves along the way.

You will see an ASPTL icon at the end of each chapter. These serve as a gentle reminder that no matter the moment you are in, no matter what life brings, there can always be a safe place to land. Sometimes that place is internal. Sometimes it is found in others. Sometimes it is created through effort, vulnerability, and patience with ourselves.

Healing is not a straight line. It is a journey made of questions, setbacks, growth, and renewed strength. My hope is that this book offers companionship on that path and reminds you that even when life feels heavy, your story is still unfolding and your landing place is still being built.

I am grateful you chose to read these pages. Take what supports you and carry it forward in your own way.

Pain is part of the journey.
Landing is part of the victory.

PREFACE

Lord, thank You for Your divine appointments, even when we don't recognize them at first. Thank You for teaching me that Your timing is perfect, even when it doesn't match our plans. Let these words be a light for someone who is walking through their own season of preparation. In Jesus' name, Amen.

> *"'For I know the plans I have for you,' declares the LORD, 'plans to prosper you and not to harm you, plans to give you hope and a future.'"*
> **Jeremiah 29:11 (NIV)**

A year ago, if you'd told me I'd be writing a book about marriage while watching mine unravel, I would've called you a liar. Yet here I am, pen in hand, heart on paper, trying to make sense of how God uses our breaking points to build testimonies.

I can already feel some of you pulling back. Maybe you picked up this book looking for marriage wisdom from someone who's "made it." Someone who could tell you about the mountain from the summit, not from the middle of the climb. Someone whose life looks more put together, whose story has a neater bow on top.

But here's what I've learned about testimony: we do ourselves — and God — a disservice when we wait until the struggle is safely behind us to speak about it. In our humanity, we have this tendency to sanitize our stories once we've survived them. We package our pain in acceptable phrases, smooth out the rough edges of our reality, forgetting that someone else might need to hear about the fight while they're still fighting.

Our testimony isn't ours to keep. It's not a private victory medal to polish and put on a shelf. It's a lifeline God means for us to throw to others who are drowning in the same storms we survived. That's why I'm writing from this raw place — from the space between what God promised and what my eyes can see.

Lately, I've been studying Lot's wife in Scripture. Her story hits different when you're standing at your own crossroads between what was and what could be. Most people remember her as that pillar of salt, a cautionary tale about the danger of looking back. But God's been showing me something deeper about her story.

See, Lot was trying to lead his family to the Promised Land just like I've been trying to lead in my marriage. But his wife couldn't release her grip on the familiar, even when the familiar was destroying her. Was it really Sodom she turned back for? Or was it the weight of uncertainty ahead that made her look behind? Sometimes the devil we know feels safer than the God we're still learning to trust.

The adversary knows our weak spots. Knows exactly when to whisper that looking back is safer than moving forward, that hardening our hearts hurts less than keeping them open to hope. After two marriages, one divorce and a second divorce underway, most men would build walls high enough to touch heaven. Some would say I've earned that right. But God keeps drawing me back to deeper truths about what marriage really means — not just a relationship between one man and one woman, but a living picture of His love for us, broken as we are.

As the weight of writing this book settled on my spirit, I found myself reminiscing over a relationship with this person that originated as friendship and organically evolved into a marriage thirty years later. Did I ever think that marriage would ever actually happen? No. But when it did, it took five years of building what I thought was unshakeable. And then, less than one year of marriage. The numbers don't add up to what I thought our story would be, but maybe that's exactly the point. Learning from my first marriage I took friendship, communication and transparency as what would sustain a meaningful relationship.

In these pages, I speak about people who once held a special place in my life — people I broke bread with, traveled alongside, and truly considered family. So when they chose sides, it cut deep. It felt as though they had never truly seen or understood the sincerity of how I loved and treated my wife.

I reached out, hoping someone might hear me, or even just acknowledge my pain — but no one did. No one spoke up for me. What hurt the most was seeing their blind loyalty as if everything I had shared and given meant nothing.

It left me feeling like my place in those relationships was conditional — that I was valued only when things were easy. When I let someone into my world, I give them my trust, my loyalty, and my commitment. That's what I want people to understand.

In the fog of pain, when everything feels like it's slipping away, it's okay to be hurt. We can act out of emotion and lose sight of ourselves for a moment. I was emotional — deeply so — and in those moments, I felt completely alone, with no one by my side.

When people tell me, "It's going to be okay," I know they mean well, but it's hard to accept because I didn't want to stop loving her, honoring her, or protecting her. Even in my fifties, I put myself in a position to change and grow because I truly loved being her husband — not just for companionship, but for devotion, commitment, and becoming the man I wanted to be for her.

When Moses led the Israelites out of Egypt, that journey to the Promised Land should have taken days, not decades. But God knew those wilderness years weren't punishment — they were preparation. Some lessons can only be learned in the desert, where distractions die and miracles become necessary for survival.

I've been thinking about that a lot lately. About how God sometimes must strip everything away before He can rebuild it His way. About how the same faith that tells me to keep praying for restoration also requires me to trust that even if restoration looks different than I imagined, God's purpose won't fail.

Marriage, as God designed it, was never meant to be what we've turned it into. Growing up, nobody in my family talked about what Godly marriage looked like. We didn't have examples of couples who stayed together, let alone thrive together. All we inherited were broken models and survival skills that don't serve us in building something sacred.

The Greek word *ekklesia* — assembly, congregation, church — keeps echoing in my spirit. Maybe because God's showing me that a marriage isn't just about two people sharing a life; it's about creating a living sanctuary where broken people can become holy together. But how do you build that kind of sacred space when your foundation feels like it's crumbling?

Some nights, I catch myself bargaining with God: *Lord, if You restore this marriage, I'll do it differently this time. I'll lead better, love harder, pray longer.* But then His Spirit whispers back: *What if this breaking is part of your building? What if this stripping away is making room for something you couldn't receive while your hands were full of your own plans?*

I think about Joseph in that pit, looking up at the stars through a hole his brothers made. I wonder if he knew then that the pit wasn't his ending — it was his preparation for purpose. That sometimes God must take you lower before He can lift you higher.

That's why I'm writing this book from the middle of my storm — in the midst of my second divorce — not from the safety of its passing. Because when you read these words right now, you are standing right where I am standing — trying to hold onto faith while your marriage feels like it's slipping through your fingers. You need to know you're not alone in this wilderness, that your breaking might just be God's building in disguise.

Don't get me wrong — this isn't a book about accepting defeat. This is about learning to trust God's process even when it hurts. About understanding that sometimes restoration doesn't look like what we prayed for, but it always looks like what we need.

PART ONE

FOUNDATIONS

CHAPTER 1

A NEW BEGINNING

(1996)

"See, I am doing a new thing! Now it springs up; do
you not perceive it? I am making a way in the wilder-
ness and streams in the wasteland."

Isaiah 43:19 (NIV)

I t was the spring of 1996. I had just graduated from college —
a milestone I had imagined countless times as the doorway to
purpose, stability, and recognition. In my mind, that degree
would be the key to unlock the life I had been working toward.
I had done what I was told to do: study hard, stay focused, avoid
too many distractions, and chase the image of success that had
been painted for me. But standing there in cap and gown, surrounded by applause and congratulations, I didn't feel trium-
phant. I felt hollow.

There was a restlessness in my chest that no celebration could
quiet. It wasn't fear, not exactly. It was more like a quiet ache.

A spiritual unease that whispered, There's more. The life I had built — the identity I had worn like armor — suddenly felt too small. I had climbed the ladder, but I wasn't even sure if it was leaning against the right wall. I wasn't drifting because I didn't have options. I was drifting because the options I had no longer excited me. They felt like echoes of someone else's expectations.

Sometimes the scariest thing God will ever ask you to do is leave a life that looks successful but no longer fits your soul.

And to make it more complicated, I wasn't lost in some unfamiliar place. I was in Oakland. Home. My streets. My people. The soil that shaped me. The city was in my bones. It had taught me how to read danger before it walked into the room. It had given me swagger, survival, and silence — the kind of silence that keeps you safe but slowly starves your soul. I knew how to move. I knew how to disappear in plain sight. Oakland taught you how to be a man, but not necessarily how to be whole.

I loved my city, but I knew it had done all it could for me. The soil that grew me couldn't sustain the version of me that was trying to break through. I wasn't abandoning my roots. I was following the whisper of destiny. The kind of whisper that doesn't shout — it stirs. It lingers. It refuses to be ignored.

Leaving wasn't heroic. It was terrifying. Everything in me wanted to cling to what was familiar. I knew the game here. I knew how to win it, how to play it safe. But something inside me was done with safety. Safety wasn't growth. It wasn't faith. It wasn't freedom. And somewhere deep in my spirit, I began to sense that God was pulling me into something unfamiliar — not to punish me, but to prepare me.

The problem was, I didn't really know who I was without the mask. Without the toughness. Without the illusion of control. For years, I'd carried around ideas of manhood that were handed down through the streets, through media, through broken men who hadn't been taught either. I thought having women made me valuable. I thought pushing people away made me strong. I thought being untouchable made me secure. But all it did was isolate me. All it did was hide the truth: I was afraid.

Afraid of not being enough. Afraid of being seen. Afraid that if I took off the mask, I wouldn't like the man underneath.

But cracks were forming. God has a way of allowing our carefully built identities to start crumbling — not to destroy us, but to deliver us. And the version of me that had been crafted out of ego, pride, pain, and survival was beginning to erode. I started catching glimpses of a man I didn't recognize but deeply wanted to become.

So, I left.

Not because I had it all figured out. But because I knew staying meant stagnation. Staying meant pretending. Staying meant shrinking into a version of myself that had already expired. I needed to go. Not just geographically, but spiritually. I needed to leave behind the stage and finally meet the man behind the curtain.

Washington, D.C., became the destination. I told people I was going for graduate school and new opportunities, but truthfully, I was searching. I didn't have a real plan. I had a stirring. I had a need for something real. Something holy. Something that would make me whole.

When I stepped off that plane in early January 1997, D.C. greeted me like a slap to the soul. The cold wasn't just uncomfortable — it was disrespectful. California boys aren't built for snow, and I had shown up with sneakers, a light jacket, and no gloves. My first week felt like punishment. The cold cut through my layers, through my pride, through my assumptions. I fell on ice more times than I'd like to admit. One morning, I slipped and hit the ground so hard I just lay there for a minute, staring at the sky and wondering if I'd made a mistake.

But God doesn't waste pain. Not even frozen fingers and bruised pride.

That first winter was more than a crash course in East Coast weather. It was my initiation into surrender. I didn't have a blueprint. I didn't have family or mentors to show me the ropes. I had instinct. I had prayer. I had quiet moments where God started whispering to the parts of me that had been silenced for too long.

I took a job at Gold's Gym on Capitol Hill. It wasn't a power move. It wasn't impressive. But it was exactly where I needed to be. The gym was filled with politicians, professionals, people chasing goals bigger than themselves. Watching them — how they trained, how they carried themselves — made me think differently. These weren't the kind of men who needed to posture. They were focused. Disciplined. Intentional. And something about that started rubbing off on me.

It was in that space — between reps and routines — that I first saw her.

Hope.

She didn't move like someone trying to be seen. She moved like someone who knew who she was. Confident. Calm. Present. Her short hair framed her face, but it was her spirit that caught me. She had that rare quality of making you want to be better, without saying a word. There was no drama. No performance. Just authenticity. And for a man who had spent years behind masks, that was magnetic.

At first, I didn't approach her. I wasn't ready. I didn't even know how to carry a conversation without putting on a show. But every time I saw her, something stirred. It wasn't just attraction. It was alignment. It was a sense that this wasn't random.

And then, one day, she disappeared. Just … gone. I felt it in the atmosphere. The gym felt emptier, like a song had stopped playing. I caught myself hoping she'd come back. I even prayed — not loud, just a whisper in my heart.

5

When she finally returned a few weeks later, I knew I couldn't miss the moment. I walked over, heart pounding, palms sweaty.

"Hey," I said. "My name's Elton. What's yours?"

She looked up, eyes steady, presence unshaken.

"Hope," she said.

A name. A word. A confirmation. In that moment, I didn't just meet a woman — I met a reflection. A glimpse of the man I was becoming.

That first season in Washington, D.C., tested me. It pulled at the foundations I had stood on for years and revealed just how fragile they were. And yet, in the testing, I was beginning to be transformed.

> *"Because you know that the testing of your faith produces perseverance. Let perseverance finish its work so that you may be mature and complete, not lacking anything."*
>
> **James 1:3–4 (NIV)**

And that was exactly what God was doing. Not punishing me. Not abandoning me. He was maturing me. Completing me. Stripping away what I had built, so He could rebuild me from the inside out.

Brother to Brother: Listen

You can look the part and still be lost. You can have a good haircut, a fresh fit, and a reputation that walks in before you do — and still be crumbling under the weight of what you refuse to face. I know, because that was me. And maybe, it's you, too.

You were taught to be hard. To chase women. To never cry. To never ask for help. You were taught that dominance was power and silence was strength. But that's not manhood. That's fear, dressed up as swagger.

Real strength? It's submission. Not to weakness — but to God. It's saying yes to transformation, even when it feels like death to your ego. It's choosing purpose over popularity. Growth over image. Healing over hiding.

Leaving what's familiar will break you — but it will also build you.

You'll fall. You'll doubt. You'll look in the mirror and not recognize who you're becoming. But keep going. Keep growing. Because the streets didn't make you — they just introduced you to your survival mode. But God? He's trying to introduce you to your purpose.

And when you meet her — the woman who walks in wholeness, peace, confidence — don't just try to impress her. Learn from her. Because she might not be your reward. She might be your mirror.

The old you had image. The new you will have impact.

So, stop performing. Stop pretending. Let God mold you.

This isn't your ending, brother. This is your beginning.

And trust me — God knows exactly what He's doing with you.

Brother to Sister: Cover His Becoming in Prayer

Sis, before he can lead you, he has to learn how to follow God. That's where your prayers come in.

Maybe you've met him already. Maybe you haven't. But right now — somewhere out there — there's a man God is shaping. He's in a season of becoming. Becoming more than just a provider. Becoming more than what the world expects. Becoming God's man. And Sis, whether you're dating him, married to him, or still waiting for him, one of the most powerful things you can do is pray for who he's becoming — not just who he is.

Because every man of God has a beginning. And it doesn't always look pretty. Sometimes he's confused. Sometimes he's stuck. Sometimes he doesn't even realize he's being prepared. That's when your intercession becomes his unseen anchor.

Pray this over him:

Lord, I lift up the man You've chosen for me — whether he's already in my life or still being prepared.

Cover him as he navigates his new beginning.

Speak louder than his doubts.

Protect him from comparison and insecurity.

Don't let him settle for less than what You've called him to.

Plant him in Your Word.

Surround him with brothers that will keep him accountable.

And when he's tired — remind him that Your strength is made perfect in weakness.

Let him find his identity in You — not in applause, not in achievements, not even in me.

Give me the patience to wait well. The wisdom to speak life.

And the grace to honor his process without trying to control it.

In Jesus' name, Amen.

Sister, remember this: Your prayers won't make him perfect. But they will make room for God to work.

BECOMING BEFORE BELONGING

Scripture Focus

> *"Before I formed you in the womb I knew you, before*
> *you were born, I set you apart."*
>
> **Jeremiah 1:5 (NIV)**

♫ Dedicated Song

"Back at One" — Brian McKnight

A soulful reflection of new beginnings and simple, intentional steps toward connection. Perfect for capturing the hopeful tone of starting again.

Reflection

New beginnings often come with questions:

- Who am I now?
- What am I supposed to do next?
- Will I ever feel whole again?

In the wake of transition — whether after graduation, heartbreak, or spiritual awakening — we often rush to redefine ourselves through achievements, relationships, or approval. But God isn't asking you to fix yourself. He's asking you to trust that He already knows who you are becoming.

This season is not just about starting over — it's about *starting honest.*

Not striving. Not performing. Just showing up in front of God with all your questions and letting Him do the shaping.

Before you seek belonging with someone else, let God show you who you are with Him. Before you chase the next opportunity, let Him anchor your identity.

Because becoming is not about *doing more* — it's about *surrendering deeper.*

Reflection Questions

1. Where are you currently looking for identity or validation?

2. What part of your past do you need to release to walk in your true identity?

3. Have you confused doing with becoming — performance with purpose?

4. What would it look like to trust God with your process, not just your outcome?

5. How has this season been shaping you in ways you didn't expect?

Prayer

Lord, thank You for new beginnings — even when they come wrapped in uncertainty.

I surrender my need to have it all figured out.

Reveal to me who I am—not through performance, but through Your presence.

Help me to become before I belong, and to walk confidently in the identity You already see.

In Jesus' name, Amen.

CHAPTER 2

THE WILDERNESS YEARS

(2016–2018)

*"Remember how the LORD your God led you all the
way in the wilderness these forty years, to humble and
test you in order to know what was in your heart ..."*

Deuteronomy 8:2 (NIV)

We often think of the wilderness as a place — somewhere dry, desolate, and detached from everything we consider familiar. But in God's design, the wilderness is never just a location. It's a process. A proving ground. It's the sacred space between what you've left behind and what you've not yet stepped into. It's where He strips away what no longer serves you, reveals what was buried beneath the surface, and begins to shape the version of you that couldn't survive in Egypt. The wilderness is not about punishment — it's about preparation.

When God led the Israelites into the wilderness, it wasn't because He was disappointed in them. It was because He loved them too much to let Egypt live on inside of them. They had left the place of bondage, but the bondage hadn't yet left them. And that's exactly how it felt for me.

I met my first wife in the fall 1998 through her sister. As she came walking down the stairs she intrigued me. She had a 2-year-old son and I viewed them as a package. Through the years I've seen men attempt to create a wedge between mother and child. That's not me and that's not how a respectable man should conduct himself. We pursued a relationship and got married in 2000 and had our daughter in 2001.

Most people, when they decide to get married, plan on it being "'til death do us part." I was no different: I believed you must get it in your heart to sustain a lifetime with someone. You should want to evolve during the test of times, as people change with age.

But in 2016, after seventeen years of marriage, we did part. The betrayal of infidelity shattered everything I had convinced myself was unshakable. A wound I never saw coming. One I didn't know how to process. It hit hard. Not just because of what happened, but because of what it exposed. It revealed cracks in the foundation we had never repaired. Pain, we had never confronted. Distance we had pretended wasn't there.

Before continuing with my story, let me be clear: despite the hurt I felt when my marriage ended, I maintain respect for my ex-wife to this day and genuinely wish her the best.

When you have the mindset of forever and betrayal has occurred, it alters a number of things as it relates to your future to what's next. I wasn't just grieving the end of a marriage. I was grieving the identity I had built around it. I was mourning the man I thought I was, the image I had fought to uphold, the version of life I thought was secure. I had worked hard to become stable, responsible, disciplined — and suddenly, all that structure felt like it was collapsing in my hands.

Before everything came undone, I saw myself as a man who had it together. Being a husband is more than just saying I do, it's willing to make sacrifices that people outside of your household would never know or understand. Those sacrifices are unconditional because of the love that's associated with it. Working jobs that you thought were beneath you and did it anyway with no one knowing the internal hurt you were enduring and the criticism that follows. Outside family members judging where you should be as opposed to where you are in that moment. But still I knew my role. I provided. I protected. I stayed consistent. I wore responsibility like a badge of honor — husband, father, leader. But when life unraveled, when the roles fell away and the titles dissolved, I was forced to confront a difficult question: Who am I now?

In the wilderness, you are forced to meet the version of yourself that can't hide behind performance. It strips you down until there's no platform to stand on, no applause to distract you, no roles left to play. It was in that silence, in that soul-stretching solitude, that I came to see how much of my identity had been built on doing instead of being. I had believed that manhood meant keeping everything together, never showing weakness, always having the answer. I had confused pressure with purpose and performance with identity. But true manhood isn't measured by how much you can carry — it's revealed in how much you're willing to surrender.

There are debts in life that don't show up on credit reports. Some are emotional. Others spiritual. And when I look back on that season, I can admit — I was bankrupt in both. I had spent so much of myself trying to be strong for everyone else that I stopped paying attention to the quiet ache inside my own soul. I thought sacrifice was noble. I thought always putting others first was the highest expression of love. And in many ways, it was. But the soul keeps the receipts. Eventually, it collects.

I was tired. Worn thin. Drained from silently carrying everyone else's weight without ever acknowledging my own needs. And in the midst of all this, I was still showing up. Still praying. Still reading the Word. But the connection had weakened. I had confused activity with intimacy. I thought doing things for God meant I was walking closely with Him. But I was busy in His name without being still in His presence. And without knowing it, I had begun to live disconnected — functioning from routine rather than relationship, surviving on fumes, mistaking momentum for meaning.

As much as the betrayal hurt, what it uncovered cut deeper. It forced me to ask questions that were as uncomfortable as they were necessary. Had I truly been present in that marriage? Had I created space for my wife to be seen and heard — or was I just physically showing up while emotionally checking out? Did I love from a place of connection, or was I simply performing the duties of a husband without offering the depth of a partner?

Infidelity rarely begins in the physical. It begins in the emotional distance, the missed conversations, the slow erosion of intimacy. I had to acknowledge that I was consistent but not always connected. I was loyal, but not always emotionally available. I thought my presence was enough. I thought showing up counted. But sometimes love without engagement still feels like absence. And the truth is, a home without heart will always echo with unmet needs.

What hurt the most wasn't just what she did — it was all the things I hadn't done. The things I left unsaid. The emotional walls I never tore down. The way I didn't lean into healing when I should've. But in that pain, God taught me a liberating truth: you can take responsibility without taking all the blame. I didn't cause the betrayal — but I had contributed to the brokenness. And true healing begins not in finger-pointing, but in owning what's yours and surrendering what's not.

Slowly, painfully, I began to see that the wilderness was not about God breaking me down — it was about Him setting me free. Free from the lie that I had to be everything to everyone. Free from the pressure to prove myself through performance. Free from the belief that my worth was tied to my role. God wasn't humiliating me — He was humbling me. He wasn't casting me aside — He was calling me deeper. He wasn't interested in refining my image — He wanted to restore my identity.

Just as Israel's forty years were not wasted but used to prepare them for promise, my own three years of stripping away were making space for something greater than what I'd lost. The wilderness was a gift I didn't want but desperately needed. I put in the work because I never wanted to experience this kind of pain ever again.

The Israelites witnessed miracles in the wilderness. Manna falling like grace from the sky. Water bursting from rocks. A cloud leading by day and fire guiding by night. And yet, even with all that evidence, they still struggled to trust. I understand that now more than ever. God was still showing up for me, too. Still providing. Still protecting. Still speaking. But I couldn't always hear Him — not because He had gone silent, but because I was still mourning what I lost instead of embracing what He was building.

Like them, I often looked back to "Egypt," missing what was familiar even if it wasn't healthy. But God was patiently pulling my gaze forward, reminding me that the promise was still ahead.

And perhaps the hardest confession a man can make is this: I can't fix it. We're wired to repair, to hold things together, to make it work. But not every fracture is a failure. Some things break because the version that existed couldn't carry the weight of what was next. Some things have to fall apart so God can rebuild them stronger, deeper, and more aligned with His design.

I fought for that marriage. I prayed, fasted, stood on Scripture, and believed for restoration. I did what I knew to do. I stayed in the gap and pleaded with heaven. But restoration doesn't always happen the way we imagine. Sometimes God allows silence. Sometimes separation. Sometimes even sorrow. Not because He's forgotten us — but because He's forming us. And in all of that God gives us the ability to make decisions and choices. Just because we have this ability doesn't always mean we make the right choices, and the outcome was divorce in 2017. People need to understand that divorce just doesn't affect two people; it affects entire families from both sides. That is the tragic reality.

Yet I believe with every part of me: God is still in the business of restoring marriages. Not just making them bearable or functional but restoring them to reflect His heart. His covenant. His power. His glory. Marriage isn't just about comfort. It's about calling. It isn't just about building a life. It's about fulfilling a purpose. And purpose often requires pressure. It requires pruning. It requires wilderness.

In Scripture, every wilderness season that ended in promise carried a testimony of transformation. Mine would be no different. What I thought was ruin was really the soil for revival.

When Jesus is at the center, what once felt like ruin becomes the soil for revival. What looked like devastation becomes the foundation for destiny. When God covers a marriage, it doesn't just survive — it thrives. It becomes a testimony of redemption and grace. A living, breathing story that points not to human perfection, but to divine faithfulness.

If you find yourself in that kind of wilderness right now — grieving, questioning, wondering how things could change so quickly — know this: God is not done. He's still writing. He's still working behind the scenes. And even though restoration may not look the way you envisioned, when God rebuilds something, it never goes back to normal. It goes forward to greater.

Brother to Brother

To the man reading this who feels like everything around you is collapsing — listen to me. You are not forgotten. You are not abandoned. And you are not finished. What you're facing right now is not the end of your story — it's the breaking open of a new beginning. This is not your failure. This is your becoming.

You are in the middle of the process. And the process, as painful as it feels, is holy. It's sacred ground. Because it's in the wilderness where God does His deepest work — not when you're strong, but when you're surrendered. He is peeling back the layers you've used to survive. The ego. The image. The need to be everything for everyone. He is stripping what was never meant to stay — not to shame you, but to save you. The pressure you feel isn't punishment — it's the hands of a loving Father molding you into the man He originally designed you to be.

This wilderness you're walking through. It's not a graveyard. It's a birthplace. This is the place where the masks fall, where the silence finally gives way to honesty, where the version of you that was performing dies so the version of you that is called can live. You're not being buried — you're being planted. And what's buried in brokenness will rise in power if you don't give up in the dark.

Let God deal with the debts — every one of them. The emotional ones that left you numb. The spiritual ones that left you distant. The financial ones that kept you up at night. The relational ones that shattered your sense of worth. He can handle what you can't. And He's not asking you to fix everything. He's asking you to trust Him with what you can no longer carry.

Because sometimes, the very place where everything falls apart is the exact place where God begins again. What feels like a breakdown may be heaven's setup for breakthrough.

So, if you're still in your wilderness — still aching, still wrestling, still searching — don't stop walking. Don't build a home in regret. Don't pitch a tent in bitterness. Don't decorate the valley. You weren't meant to die there. Keep moving. Keep pressing. Keep believing. The fire is refining you. The silence is shaping you. The pain is producing purpose.

You are not just being tested. You are being transformed.

Let perseverance finish its work. Let God finish what He started. And when the dust settles, you won't just be healed — you'll be whole. You'll be wise. You'll be rooted.

> *"Let perseverance finish its work so that you may be mature and complete, not lacking anything."*
>
> **James 1:4 (NIV)**

There is life on the other side of this.

There is purpose in the middle of this.

There is a promise beyond what you've lost.

So, keep walking. God's not done.

Brother to Sister: Pray Through His Wilderness

Sis, every man walks through a wilderness season — a time when everything he thought he knew gets tested, when what once made sense falls apart, and when God starts dealing with what no one else can see.

He may not talk about it. He may try to act like he's fine. But deep down, he's wrestling. With failure. With identity. With the weight of who he thought he'd be by now. The wilderness doesn't mean he's lost. It means God is doing deep work — and deep work takes time.

So, don't just pray for the version of him who shows up strong. Pray for the version who feels like quitting but keeps showing up anyway.

Your prayers won't pull him out of the wilderness prematurely — but they can give him strength to keep walking through it.

Pray this over him:

Lord, I lift up the man who feels like he's walking through a dry, silent place.

Strip away everything that's not from You — false strength, pride, performance, shame.

Show him that the wilderness isn't where You abandoned him — it's where You're rebuilding him.

When he questions who he is, whisper truth into his soul.

When he feels like giving up, remind him that surrender is not the same as defeat.

Help me not to judge his silence, but to stand in the gap for him.

Give me eyes to see the calling behind the chaos.

Teach me how to pray, not out of fear, but from a place of faith.

I trust You with his process.

I trust You with the fire.

I trust You with the man.

In Jesus' name, Amen.

WHEN GOD FEELS SILENT

Scripture Focus

> *"He led you through the vast and dreadful wilderness … to humble and test you so that in the end it might go well with you."*
>
> **Deuteronomy 8:15–16 (NIV)**

♫ Dedicated Song

"Rescue" — Lauren Daigle

This song captures the raw emotion of walking through a wilderness season — when everything familiar falls away and you're left face to face with your brokenness and your God.

Reflection

The wilderness isn't punishment — it's preparation.

In this season, everything familiar may fall apart. People leave. Plans crumble. God seems distant. But beneath the silence is a God who is closer than ever, pruning you for purpose.

The wilderness is where idols are exposed. Where control is surrendered. Where your heart gets rewired to beat in sync with heaven, not with fear or desire. You may cry out and hear nothing, but He hears every whisper. He sees every tear. And He's not just working on your situation — He's working on you.

You may not recognize yourself on the other side of the wilderness. That's the point. God isn't trying to restore the old version of you. He's birthing something new — stronger, wiser, surrendered.

Reflection Questions

1. What false comforts did the wilderness season expose in your life?

2. How has God's silence forced you to confront your real identity?

3. In what ways have you grown spiritually during seasons of isolation?

4. What are you learning about obedience without outcomes?

5. How would your faith look if you stopped trying to exit the wilderness and started asking God what it's for?

Prayer

Father, I don't always understand the silence, but I trust You in it. Help me not to run from the wilderness, but to receive everything You're trying to teach me. Refine me until I reflect You. In Jesus' name, Amen.

CHAPTER 3

GOD'S CALLING

(2018)

"Being confident of this, that he who begun a good work in you will carry it on to completion until the day of Jesus Christ."

(Philippians 1:6)

Sometimes we think we've closed the door on a chapter, only to discover later that God was still writing the next sentence. And sometimes, the sentence He writes in the dark becomes the very light that leads you home. That's what 2018 became for me — a slow, quiet continuation of a story I thought had ended with a slammed door and shattered dreams. I had convinced myself that my role in love, in marriage, in companionship was over. I wasn't angry. I wasn't bitter. But I was exhausted. And from that exhaustion, I made a vow that I thought would protect me: *Never again.*

The pain from my divorce in 2017 hadn't just cut deep — it had reached into the marrow of who I was. It was more than the collapse of a relationship. It was the death of an identity I had been proud to wear for 17 years. Husband. Protector. Leader. I had wrapped those words around my soul like a second skin. I had worked hard, prayed faithfully, remained committed even when things didn't make sense. And yet, I watched what I had fought for slip through my fingers.

It felt like God had gone silent. I would wake up, go through the motions, keep the faith publicly, and yet inside, I felt spiritually muted. I was still praying — but those prayers felt like they were bouncing off the ceiling. I was still reading my Bible — but the words weren't lighting the same fire they once had. I was still going to church — but the worship didn't reach me the way it used to.

I had become proficient in spiritual activity while quietly suffocating under emotional weight. The disappointment was layered, not just from the relationship that ended, but from the quiet feeling that maybe I had failed in ways I couldn't fully see. And so, I made a silent vow: no more. No more vulnerability. No more risk. No more building a future with someone only to watch it burn down. If I could just stay in my lane, do good, love God, serve others, and stay alone, maybe I could avoid ever feeling that kind of pain again.

I didn't even realize how tightly I had wrapped myself in that false sense of control. I convinced myself that I had peace, when really, I had only accepted resignation. I told myself that I had surrendered it to God, but in reality, I had hidden it from Him. There's a difference between laying something at God's feet and locking it away in the attic of your soul and saying, *Don't go in there.*

But God — loving, persistent, and patient — never stops pursuing the parts of us we're trying hardest to protect. It wasn't a thunderclap or a prophetic dream that broke through my wall. It was something quieter. Subtle. A whisper in the rhythm of everyday life. At first, it was a nudge. A restlessness. I couldn't explain it. Nothing dramatic had changed, but I could feel something shifting inside of me. Little things began to stir. I'd see a couple praying together or a father dancing with his daughter, and instead of cynicism, I felt a longing I thought I had buried. I'd hear sermons about restoration and instead of rolling my eyes, I'd find myself wondering: *Could that still be true for me?*

I tried to dismiss it at first. I chalked it up to emotions, to loneliness, to wishful thinking. But the whispers didn't leave. In fact, they grew louder — not externally, but internally. I started to hear this phrase rise again and again in my heart: *You haven't missed your calling. You've just misunderstood the process.*

That sentence began to unearth something in me. I had believed that because the marriage ended, the calling ended, too. That my disqualification had already been stamped and filed away in heaven. But God was trying to tell me that He hadn't changed

His mind. The pain didn't cancel the purpose. The divorce didn't dissolve the design. What I saw as failure, God saw as formation.

Still, it took me time to face it. I had to wrestle with questions I didn't want to answer. And one night, as I sat alone in my apartment — no music playing, no TV on, no distractions — I found myself staring out the window, asking the question I had suppressed for so long: *God ... do You still want me to be a husband?*

Just asking it brought tears to my eyes. Not because I was ready, but because I finally admitted that deep down, I still longed for what I had sworn off. And that's when the real conversation with God began. Not the polished one. Not the surface-level one. But the raw, unfiltered one. I said, *Lord, if You still want that for me — if that role is still part of my story — then I don't want it unless it's from You. I don't want a repeat. I don't want recycled pain. I want purpose. And if that means You have to break me to rebuild me, then do it.*

That prayer didn't unlock immediate answers, but it opened the gate to a refining process I wasn't prepared for. The first thing God did was ask me a question I didn't see coming. In the stillness of my spirit, I heard Him ask, *Were you a bad husband?* I didn't hesitate. *No,* I said. *I was faithful. I provided. I protected. I did what I thought I was supposed to do.* And it was true. I had done what I thought was right.

But then came the follow-up question, and it pierced through every justification I had built: *But did you submit your role as a husband to Me?*

That question didn't just challenge my actions — it exposed my heart. The truth? No. I hadn't submitted it. I had led based on my understanding, my instincts, and even my good intentions — but I hadn't led from a place of surrender. I hadn't invited God to lead *me* as I led *her*. I had asked for His help but not His Lordship. I had done marriage my way, with His blessing in the background but not His voice in the center.

That realization broke me.

I began to see that I had treated marriage like a job instead of a calling. Like a task to complete instead of a mission to embody. And God began to slowly, gently, dismantle that mindset. He didn't condemn me. He didn't shame me. He simply began to rebuild me. From the inside out.

What followed was not a season of dating or romantic desire — it was a season of divine refinement. God started teaching me what true headship looked like. It wasn't about being in control — it was about being under authority. It wasn't about having the final say — it was about listening to God's voice first. He began to show me that loving someone well means leading them with humility, serving them with patience, and covering them with grace. It means being a safe place. A steady place. A surrendered place.

My desires began to shift. I no longer wanted just a wife — I longed for a marriage that would reflect God's heart. Not something based on compatibility or surface connection, but on covenant. On calling. On a mission. I didn't want a relationship that just worked — I wanted a relationship that *worshiped*.

So, I waited. But not in the way I had before. This was not passive waiting. This was not isolation disguised as holiness. This was active, expectant, faithful preparation. I prayed — not just for the woman I would one day meet, but for the man I was becoming. I prayed for her strength, her healing, her peace. I asked God to heal the wounds in her just as He was healing the wounds in me. I began preparing my heart not for a person, but for a purpose.

And yes — there were lonely nights. There were days I wondered if I was just romanticizing something that was never going to happen again. There were whispers of doubt, echoes of past failure, reminders of what didn't work before. But deeper than all of that, there was peace. Not peace that came from knowing the future, but peace that came from trusting the One who holds it.

Looking back now, I understand that what I thought was the end was actually the beginning of a holy transformation. God wasn't punishing me — He was purifying me. He wasn't rejecting me — He was rebuilding me. He had to break my pride, strip my self-reliance, and quiet the noise of my own voice so I could finally hear His. And in that stillness, in that fire, in that slow, sacred process, He was forging something eternal in me.

He was preparing me to love again. Not from my wounds, but from my healing. Not from my past, but from my purpose. And when He decides the time is right — when He sees that I am truly ready, not just desiring but surrendered — He will trust me again with what my heart was made to carry.

And this time, I'll carry it differently. I won't carry it from fear, or ego, or survival. I'll carry it from the overflow of grace that only comes from being forged in the fire of God's love.

Brother to Brother: You Didn't Miss It

Brother, if you've ever stood in the fire of a broken marriage … If you've stared at the ashes of what you thought would last forever … If you've ever made a quiet vow in the darkness of your pain, promising never to let anyone close again — I see you. I understand. I've been there.

I know what it's like to give everything you have — to pray, to lead, to stay faithful — and still watch it fall apart. I know the pain of trying to hold a covenant together with hands that are bleeding from the effort. I know the silence that follows after the door closes for the last time. That deafening silence that makes you question not just what went wrong — but whether you were ever enough to begin with.

And maybe, like me, you've wondered if God could still use you. *After the divorce. After the disappointment. After the detour.*

You wonder if the calling is still intact or if the pain disqualified you. You wonder if you missed your moment — if everything you believed in was just a beautiful dream that died too soon.

But hear me, Brother: You didn't miss your calling. You just misunderstood the process.

God never throws away broken men — He refines them. He doesn't waste pain — He transforms it.

And just because something ended doesn't mean *you're* finished.

I used to think I had fallen out of favor because of what I endured. But now I understand — I wasn't being punished. I was being prepared.

God had to break the pride I didn't know I was carrying. He had to strip away the false security I had built around roles and routines. He had to silence the noise — so I could finally hear His voice again.

The wilderness wasn't where I lost myself. It's where I found my identity — not as a husband, not as a provider, but as a son. It's where I learned that leadership in the home starts with surrender before God. It's where I stopped performing and started becoming.

So now, I pray different. I wait different. I lead different. Because I'm not chasing perfection anymore — I'm pursuing presence. And I've learned that real strength doesn't come from control. It comes from compassion. It comes from laying your life down like Christ did for the Church.

If you're in a season of waiting — don't waste it. Don't use it to numb the pain. Use it to let God rebuild the man you were always meant to be.

Pray for her. The woman you haven't met yet. The woman you lost. The woman you're still believing God to restore.

Pray for her not just to be ready ... but for *you* to be ready — ready to love with grace, to lead with humility, and to protect with prayer. Because this isn't just about marriage. It's about mission.

Your healing is part of your preparation. And the process may feel like fire — but it's the fire that forges the vessel. Don't rush it. Don't resent it. And whatever you do — don't walk away from the call.

Because when God sees that you are truly ready — not just with open hands, but with a surrendered heart — He will trust you again with what your heart was made to carry.

So, rise up, man of God. Wipe the dust from your face. Lift your eyes again. You are not finished. You are being forged.

Brother to Sister: Pray for His Yes to God

Sis, there will come a moment when the man God has for you is faced with a calling that will change everything — not just for him, but for you, for your future family, for generations. That moment won't always look supernatural. Sometimes, it'll show up in the middle of his routine. In a quiet prompting. In a job that doesn't fit anymore. In a restlessness that won't go away.

That's when your prayers matter most.

Pray that when God calls, he hears. And more than that — pray that he obeys. Because the enemy doesn't just fear the man he is right now. He fears the man he'll become once he says yes to heaven.

Pray this over him:

Lord, I pray for the moment he hears You — whether it's loud or subtle, clear or confusing.

Don't let him ignore the call.

Don't let him settle for safe when You're calling him into something greater.

Give him the courage to say yes — even if it costs him comfort.

Even if it means walking away from something good to follow something God.

Break any lie that says he's not ready.

Silence the noise of fear, doubt, and delay.

Surround him with voices that speak faith and vision.

Help me support the calling, not compete with it.

Teach me to pray for his purpose, not just my preference.

When the world says he should play it safe —

Let him follow You instead.

In Jesus' name, Amen.

HIDDEN, BUT NOT FORGOTTEN

Scripture Focus

> *"He made my mouth like a sharpened sword, in the shadow of His hand He hid me; He made me into a polished arrow and concealed me in His quiver."*
>
> **Isaiah 49:2 (NIV)**

♬ Dedicated Song

"Refiner" — Maverick City Music

A soul-piercing cry for God to purify and shape you in the fire of wilderness — authentic and powerful.

Reflection

There are seasons when God hides you — not to punish you, but to protect you. To prepare you.

You may look around and see others being celebrated, restored, or recognized, while you sit in silence. Alone. Unseen. But what if this hiddenness is holy? What if this is where the real healing happens?

David was anointed king but then sent back to the fields. Joseph had dreams of leadership but was thrown into prison. Even Jesus spent thirty years in obscurity before stepping into public ministry.

God does His best shaping in secret. He's removing the residue of past wounds. Teaching you to rely not on people's applause, but on His presence. Hiding is not rejection — it's refinement.

Reflection Questions

1. Where are you currently looking for identity or validation?

2. What part of your past do you need to release in order to walk in your true identity?

3. Have you confused doing with becoming — performance with purpose?

4. What would it look like to trust God with your process, not just your outcome?

5. How has this season been shaping you in ways you didn't expect?

Prayer

Father, thank You for hiding me when I didn't even know I needed protection. Help me to stop craving the spotlight and start trusting the shaping. Refine my heart in the quiet. Restore my soul in the shadows. And when the time is right, release me into what You've prepared — for Your glory, not mine. In Jesus' name, Amen.

PART TWO

DIVINE RECONNECTION

CHAPTER 4

THE RETURN

(JULY 2019)

"May the Lord repay you for what you have done. May
you be richly rewarded by the Lord, the God of Israel,
under whose wings you have come to take refuge."

Ruth 2:12 (NIV)

The prompt that shifted everything.

I wasn't looking for Hope — not emotionally, not spiritually, not relationally. She wasn't on my radar. I wasn't lying awake at night praying for a reunion. There were no secret petitions lifted in quiet moments, no hidden longing wrapped in prayer language. I had long since made peace with the silence that followed our separation as friends. We lost connection and life just took us on different phases of life and journeys for a season. Whatever we had, whatever it was meant to be — it had passed. Or so I thought.

Twenty years had gone by. Our stories had unfolded on separate paths. The doors had closed, not with a dramatic slam, but with a quiet finality. The kind that doesn't echo but settles. The kind you learn to live with. I had released her, released the questions, and released the weight of what never was. I wasn't bitter. I wasn't chasing restoration. I was simply … settled. Life was still. Predictable. Emotionally quiet.

God's whispers rarely break into chaos — they slip into the middle of your routine and change everything.

It was just another Tuesday morning in late July. I had just finished breakfast and was sitting in the kitchen, half-watching the news, half-mentally reviewing the day's to-do list. I was scraping the last of the eggs from my plate, preparing to clean up, when something stirred deep within me. It was subtle, yet unmistakable — a nudge in my spirit, not from memory or emotion, but something holy. Something I didn't summon and couldn't shake. A whisper without sound. A divine interruption.

Look her up.

I paused, stunned. That wasn't me. That wasn't something I thought up. That wasn't longing. That wasn't loneliness. That was the Holy Spirit. I had walked with God long enough to recognize when something internal was coming from somewhere higher. It wasn't loud or dramatic. It was quiet. But clear. So clear that ignoring it would have felt like disobedience.

Still, I hesitated — not because I feared the outcome, but because I couldn't imagine the reason. Why would I look her up now? What would that accomplish? I wasn't looking to rekindle anything. I had no hidden agenda, no desire to chase what God had closed. And yet, that prompting persisted. It wasn't nostalgia. It wasn't curiosity. It was something else. Something sacred.

So, I opened my phone and clicked on Facebook — a platform I barely used anymore, a dusty attic of old memories. It felt foreign, unnecessary. But obedience sometimes leads you through old doors for new purposes. And at exactly 11:25 a.m. on July 30, 2017, I typed a simple, unassuming message:

Hey, Hope, it's been a long time. Let's reconnect.

No plan. No strategy. Just obedience in its purest form.

To my surprise, she responded within a short amount of time. A few lines of casual pleasantries turned into exchanged numbers. What started as a check-in turned into a conversation. And what began as surface-level small talk quickly revealed undercurrents of something deeper — something neither of us expected, but both recognized. There was no flirtation. No forced chemistry. It was something sacred. Holy ground, wrapped in casual language.

We agreed to meet for lunch at Tunnicliff's Tavern, a quiet place on Capitol Hill — one she had often visited for work. It was familiar to her but new to me, yet even the location felt appointed. I arrived early, not because I was eager, but because something in me felt the weight of the moment before it even unfolded. I told myself this was just a reconnection. A simple conversation. No pressure. No expectations. Just lunch. Just catching up.

But when she walked through the door, I felt something shift. It wasn't attraction, although she looked beautiful — flowing sundress, sunglasses, and that unmistakable smile I hadn't seen in years. It wasn't nostalgia, though the history we shared quietly walked in with her. It was recognition.

There was a stillness in her presence. A peace that radiated from within. She looked like a woman who had been in the presence of God. She moved with grace. Not the kind you perform, but the kind that's been formed in fire. I saw it. I felt it. And in that moment, something eternal stirred in me — not a rush of romance, but a deep sense of spiritual familiarity. As if I wasn't meeting someone from my past — I was encountering someone God had transformed for a purpose I couldn't yet comprehend.

We sat down and started talking. But it didn't feel like catching up. It felt like rediscovery. For more than three hours, we shared our journeys — every detour, every disappointment, every lesson from the wilderness. We laid our stories bare. There were no facades. No masks. Just two people who had walked through fire and still bore the scent of grace. I listened to her words, but more than that — I listened to her heart. And in the depth of her transparency, I felt something awaken.

At one point, I leaned forward, looked her in the eyes, and said something that I hadn't rehearsed — but couldn't hold back.

"I live with no regrets. If I swing for the fences and miss, so be it. But you'll never be able to say I didn't try. I want to know you, I mean really know you."

That wasn't game. That wasn't some well-crafted line. That was faith speaking. That was obedience stepping forward, even without full understanding. That was the kind of courage that only comes when you've lost before and learned how to trust again anyway.

As I sat across from her in that booth, my mind drifted to the story of Ruth and Boaz. I remembered how Boaz didn't just see Ruth — he *recognized* her. He wasn't captivated by beauty alone. He was moved by her story, by her faith, by her journey. And I saw that same weight in Hope. She wasn't the same woman I had once known. She was deeper. More grounded. More surrendered. And something in me knew — we weren't stepping into each other's stories; we were stepping into a story that God had already been writing long before either of us realized.

Two years to the day after I sent that message — July 30, 2019 — I found myself scrolling back to it. Staring at those eight words. I was overwhelmed. Not just by what had unfolded in two years, but by the way God orchestrated every detail. Every delay. Every detour. Every day we spent not speaking had been filled with quiet preparation. And now I could see it clearly — God hadn't just reunited us. He had *refined* us first. He had worked on us individually so that we could be ready collectively.

I texted a few of my brothers in Christ that day. I shared what God had done, not to boast, but to testify. I wrote, "God never prepares you out of boredom. Every pruning has a purpose. Every delay has an address. Expect His Word over your life to find its target."

Sometimes, obedience is loud and public. But most of the time, it's quiet. It looks like pressing "send" on a message you never planned to write. It looks like showing up to lunch without a plan, but with a heart willing to listen. It looks like trusting God's timing, even when nothing makes sense. And when God says *now*, you realize the ordinary was sacred all along.

What I learned in that season reshaped the way I saw relationships forever. The world sees love as a contract — a temporary agreement based on mutual benefit. But God sees love through the lens of covenant — something binding, something holy, something that doesn't break when it's tested. Ecclesiastes says a cord of three strands is not easily broken. And I knew that if God was truly in the center, we wouldn't need to force anything. What He joins together cannot be easily undone.

That day marked more than a reconnection. It marked a resurrection. Something that once felt buried had quietly been kept alive in the heart of God. And when the time was right, He breathed on it again — not for my sake, or hers, but for His glory.

And so, if you find yourself in a waiting season — if you're clinging to a promise with trembling hands, unsure if God has forgotten your name — I encourage you to pause. Lean in. Listen. He often speaks through the mundane. Through errands. Through conversations. Through unlikely platforms like Facebook. And when He prompts you, even if it makes no sense, respond. Because it's not the size of the step that moves heaven — it's the faith behind it.

Trust the whisper. Press send. Say yes. Because when God says *now*, you won't need a blueprint. You'll just need obedience.

Brother to Brother: When God Says Now

Brother, I know what it means to protect your heart behind thick walls. To silence your own desire because you've convinced yourself the chapter is closed. To stand in the aftermath of a love once sacred and say, "It's done." To bury the hope of restoration so deep that even prayer avoids the subject — because letting go feels more righteous than believing again.

But let me tell you something I had to learn the hard way: Just because you let go doesn't mean God did.

Just because you moved forward doesn't mean God stopped writing.

Sometimes, the most life-altering shift won't come through planning, advice, or confirmation. It won't show up in strategy sessions or long talks with mentors. It comes in something quieter — something sacred.

A whisper.

A nudge.

A divine moment that makes no sense in the natural ... until heaven reveals its purpose.

I wasn't searching for reconciliation. I wasn't waiting for a sign. I wasn't chasing what once was. I was simply obeying a soft, unfamiliar instruction from the Holy Spirit. One that didn't come with clarity, only conviction. One that sounded like: *Send the message.*

And that one act — simple, small, obedient — shifted the trajectory of my life in a way only God could orchestrate.

You don't have to know what comes next. You don't need a reply. You don't need to know if the door will open or if the silence will remain. You just need to move — when God says *now*.

Because when He speaks, He's not inviting you to understand. He's inviting you to trust.

Maybe it's a text. Maybe it's a phone call. Maybe it's showing up somewhere your pride told you to avoid. Maybe it's risking your dignity for something bigger than your feelings.

And yes, maybe it looks foolish to the world. But obedience rarely makes sense — until it becomes your testimony.

Brother, don't let fear muzzle your obedience. Don't let disappointment rewrite your courage. And don't let pride keep you standing still when heaven is calling you forward.

You may not know what will happen. But I promise you, God does.

And whether she answers or doesn't, whether reconciliation comes or not, your obedience still matters. Because this isn't just about her. It's about you, becoming the man God is forming through surrender.

So lean in. Listen carefully.

When the whisper comes — move.

When the nudge comes — respond.

And when God says *now* — step out, even if it feels like you're stepping onto nothing. Because if God is in it … then you're not stepping onto nothing — you're stepping into everything.

Obedience may look like weakness to others. But in the kingdom, it's strength.

It's power. It's faith in motion.

So, stand firm. Say yes to the whisper. And trust the God who doesn't just see the moment — but the miracle behind it.

Brother to Sister:
Pray Over His Obedience to God's Timing

Sis, sometimes love doesn't come when it's convenient. Sometimes it comes when he's not looking for it at all — when he's focused on God, healing from his past, or simply living his life. And in that quiet space, God might speak. Not with lightning, not with a megaphone — but with a whisper that changes everything.

Your prayers matter in that moment.

Not to rush it. Not to force it. But to cover him so he can recognize God's voice when it calls him to move. Because sometimes the entire course of his life — and yours — hinges on whether or not he obeys that gentle nudge.

Pray this over him:

Lord, I pray for the man who's learning to follow Your voice, even when it doesn't make sense.

Teach him to trust the whisper.

Teach him to pause, to listen, to obey.

When You say reach out, let him not hesitate.

When You say look again, let him not second-guess.

Protect him from the noise of the past.

Free him from the fear of repeating old pain.

Position his heart to recognize what's from You — especially when it doesn't come in the package he expected.

If I'm part of what You're leading him to, let my heart be in alignment.

If I'm not, give me peace to keep praying anyway.

I release the timing.

I release the outcome.

But I'll never stop covering him.

In Jesus' name, Amen.

THE RETURN

(JULY 2019)

Scripture Focus

> *"I will repay you for the years the locusts have eaten — the great locust and the young locust, the other locusts and the locust swarm — my great army that I sent among you."*
>
> **Joel 2:25 (NIV)**

♫ Dedicated Song

"Best Part" — Daniel Caesar feat. H.E.R.

Smooth and reflective, it captures the awe of rediscovering someone meant for you — a love that feels orchestrated, not random.

Reflection

Sometimes, God's greatest miracles begin with the smallest acts of obedience.

You weren't looking for a breakthrough. You weren't expecting a moment of divine interruption. But then He whispered something simple: Reach out. Look again. Send the message. And something shifted.

The beauty of obedience is that it doesn't require full understanding — only faith. When God nudged you to reconnect with someone from your past, it wasn't about nostalgia. It was about divine timing. Alignment. Purpose. And a chance to walk into something holy, not familiar.

God sees the full story. You only saw the chapter you were in. But when you moved on His word, you stepped into something sacred — something only He could orchestrate.

Reflection Questions

1. Have I ever felt God prompting me to reach out or take a step I didn't fully understand?

2. What held me back — fear, pride, uncertainty, timing?

3. How do I know when it's God's voice and not just my own thoughts?

4. What blessings or relationships in my life have come from small acts of obedience?

5. Am I obeying with expectation — or trusting without conditions?

Prayer

Lord, help me to hear Your voice above all others. Give me the courage to obey You, even when the path doesn't make sense. I trust that You are writing a story bigger than I can see. Let me never underestimate the power of one obedient step. In Jesus' name, Amen.

CHAPTER 5

EARLY DAYS

(AUGUST–NOVEMBER 2019)

"Therefore, as God's chosen people, holy and dearly loved, clothe yourselves with compassion, kindness, humility, gentleness and patience."

Colossians 3:12 (NIV)

When Hope and I began dating, it didn't feel like we were starting something new. It felt like we had stepped into something that had already been written — a divine script unfolding before us. There was a rhythm to it that couldn't be explained by logic or timing. Everything moved swiftly, but not recklessly. There was peace. There was purpose. There was a steady undercurrent that let me know this wasn't infatuation. It was orchestration. Every interaction carried weight. Every conversation echoed something eternal. It felt as if heaven had already approved what was beginning to grow between us.

We weren't chasing moments of emotional high. We were pursuing something holy. We didn't go out of our way to impress each other. We simply made space to be real with one another. We spent long hours together, not in flashy restaurants or picture-perfect places, but on quiet military bases — places that many wouldn't consider romantic, but to us, they were sacred. The steady crunch of gravel under our footsteps mixed with the faint hum of flagpoles clinking in the wind. The smell of cut grass lingered in the air, and the visual quietness and structure only a military base can give, reminders of discipline and order framing our conversations. Controlled and peaceful. These spaces gave us room to slow down and see each other clearly, without the noise of the world rushing in. We walked. We talked. We sat still. And in those still moments, something extraordinary began to take shape.

From the start, our connection was grounded in friendship. We shared stories from our pasts — some beautiful, some broken. We opened up about our faith journeys, about where we had stumbled, where we had grown, and what we were still healing from. Hope didn't shrink back from truth, but she never wielded it as a weapon. Her honesty didn't wound — it healed. She had a way of speaking that made me reflect deeper and rise higher. Her words carried wisdom. Her presence carried peace. She didn't demand change — she inspired it. I wasn't just dating a woman. I was walking with someone who called out the best in me without even trying.

As we built the foundation of our relationship, it wasn't only the day-to-day moments that mattered. It was the bigger steps — the ones that stretched our trust and deepened our bond. One of those came in November 2019, when we set out on a nineteen-hour drive to Louisiana to spend Thanksgiving with my mom. Those thirty-eight hours on the road, there and back, were more than just miles of highway. They were hours of laughter, prayer, quiet reflection, and conversations that seemed to braid our souls together. In that confined space of just the two of us, Hope entrusted herself fully to me, and I carried that trust carefully. Somewhere along that endless stretch of road, we discovered a rhythm — an ease between us — that made everything feel lighter, safer, stronger.

One of the most memorable parts of those early days was how I wanted to show her how special she was to me. I found these Bond Touch bracelets — little devices that let us send a gentle vibration to each other with a tap. We created our own secret codes — two taps meant *I love you,* a long press meant *Call me now,* and it was the kind of thoughtful gesture that she told me was one of the most considerate gifts she'd ever received. For me, it was just another way of letting her know that I wanted to love her differently, intentionally, in the way I felt God had called me to.

I knew early on that she was different. And I told her so. "One day, I'm going to marry you," I said — not as a line, but as a declaration. And I meant it. But even more than wanting to marry her, I wanted to be her *last first*. Her last first date. Her last first kiss. Her last first *I love you*. I didn't want to just take her hand. I wanted to cover her heart.

Not long after we began dating, I received a clear word from the Lord: *Do not become sexually intimate before marriage.* The message came with weight. It wasn't born out of fear — it was born out of love. God wasn't trying to withhold something from me. He was trying to protect something sacred within us. I wrote the instruction down, though I later misplaced the note. But I never forgot the conviction. It stayed with me. It anchored me. And when I shared it with Hope, she didn't flinch. She honored it. She didn't just agree — she embodied it.

There were no games between us. No manipulation. No blurred lines. We went on walks at National Harbor, laughing under city lights. We'd stop by MGM just to enjoy the music, the views, the moment. And at the end of the night, I'd walk her to the door and say goodnight. No kisses. No lingering touches. I wasn't even allowed past the foyer. And as challenging as it sometimes was, deep down I knew this wasn't restriction — it was reverence. This was God setting the tone for a relationship He was writing.

But even relationships rooted in divine purpose are not exempt from temptation. One afternoon, I cooked lunch — chili, to be exact — and Hope came over. The night was soft. The atmosphere was intimate. We talked, we laughed, we drew close. And slowly, that closeness gave way to desire. Emotion began to rise. I gave in to the moment, left to buy condoms, and convinced myself that maybe this was the time to take the next step.

But when I returned, everything had shifted. I couldn't perform. My body wouldn't cooperate. Something inside me had shut down. Embarrassed, confused, and frustrated, I sat there wrestling with the weight of disappointment. I quoted Scripture out of context — "If a man doesn't work, he doesn't eat" — and refused to touch the meal I had prepared. I was angry. Not at Hope. Not even at God. I was angry at myself. Angry that I had crossed a line, even in thought. Angry that I had tried to shortcut something God was trying to sanctify.

But what I thought was failure turned out to be Fatherly intervention. God had stepped in. Not to punish me — but to protect me. That moment wasn't a condemnation. It was a rescue. A redirection. A reminder that obedience doesn't just preserve purity — it secures promise.

Hope didn't shame me. She stood beside me. She didn't use that moment to question our foundation — she used it to strengthen our commitment. Together, we reset. We prayed. We realigned. And from that moment forward, we recommitted ourselves to the path God had laid out before us. Because when God speaks something over your relationship, He doesn't just release the word — He covers it. Even when we falter, He remains faithful.

Hope wasn't just a woman I loved. She was a woman on assignment. A woman of prayer. A woman of wisdom. She didn't push me toward pleasure — she pulled me toward purpose. She wasn't moved by charm — she was anchored in calling. She made me want to become the man God had always intended me to be.

We attended church weekly, prayed together every night, and submitted our relationship to God's timing, not our own emotions. Hope helped me see that love wasn't just a feeling. It was a form of discipleship. It wasn't about what we got from each other — it was about how we honored God through each other.

That's the kind of woman a man should pray for. One who challenges you with grace, walks with you in purpose, and pulls you closer to the heart of God. I didn't just find someone I could build a life with. I found someone who made me want to build it on the Rock.

Brother to Brother: Guard the Gift

If God brings a relationship into your life that feels different ... that feels sacred ... that carries peace instead of pressure and alignment instead of confusion — don't mishandle it. Guard it like the treasure it is. Not with control or pride, but with intentionality and reverence. Because not every connection is covenant, but when God places His hand on something, you'll know.

You'll feel the weight of it in your spirit, not just the butterflies in your stomach.

If you meet a woman who draws you closer to God ... who respects your boundaries and protects your purity ... who speaks life into your spirit and challenges you to grow — don't treat her like an option. That's not just attraction. That's assignment. And assignments must be stewarded.

But understand this: even when something is God-ordained, it doesn't mean it'll be temptation-free. In fact, the more purpose a relationship carries, the more pressure it will face. The real test won't be how much you feel for her — it'll be how well you honor God in the way you lead, cover, and love her. That's where spiritual maturity is revealed.

There will be moments when your body wants to lead but your spirit says wait. Nights when everything in you says *this is the moment* — but heaven is saying *not yet*. And in those moments, the enemy will whisper lies that sound like logic: *It's okay, you love her. Marriage is coming anyway, what's the difference?*

But obedience *is* the difference.

It's what separates a relationship that just looks good from one that's truly blessed. When you choose purity over passion, when you choose prayer over pressure, when you choose discipline over desire — that's when you invite God to dwell in the middle of your love story.

And if you've already crossed lines? Listen closely: *Grace is not gone.*

You haven't disqualified yourself. You're not too far removed from God's redirection. Don't let guilt keep you from grace. Repent. Reset. Rebuild. God doesn't shame you — He shapes you. And if He's still speaking to you about it, it means He hasn't given up on what He started in you.

This isn't just about protecting her body — it's about guarding her calling.

It's not about impressing her with charm — it's about covering her in prayer.

It's not about leading with emotion — it's about leading with spiritual vision.

So, here's what I've learned, Brother, and I say it to you straight:

- **If you're single** — Build your character before you chase chemistry. Become the man you're asking God to trust with His daughter.

- **If you're dating** — Set the tone. Lead with prayer, not just plans. Establish boundaries that don't just protect her body but preserve her purpose.

- **If you've messed up** — Don't stay stuck in shame. Come boldly to grace. Learn. Grow. Try again.

- **And no matter what season you're in** — Keep your ears tuned to God's voice, especially when your flesh is loud.

One day, when you're standing at the altar, you won't just want beautiful memories — you'll want a clean conscience. You'll want to look her in the eyes and know, deep in your soul, *we didn't do everything perfectly ... but we did it God's way.*

And that, my brother, is the foundation of a love that lasts — not just in this life, but one that reflects eternity.

Brother to Sister: Pray Over the Foundation

Sis, the early days of love are delicate. Exciting, yes. But also, fragile. That's when emotions rise fast and clarity can get clouded. That's when the enemy tries to tempt him to move too quickly, compromise too soon, or lean into desire more than discipline. And that's when your prayers become critical.

Not just that he falls for you, but that he honors God while doing it.

Pray that the foundation he builds in this season won't crumble when storms hit later. Pray that his pursuit is led by the Spirit, not just chemistry. Because how a man starts says a lot about how he'll lead.

Pray this over him:

Lord, I pray for the man at the start of something new — something holy.

Guard his mind.

Guard his eyes.

Guard his emotions.

Let him pursue with intention, not impulse.

Let him see me in the Spirit before he sees me through the lens of the flesh.

Let him be led by You, not his feelings.

I pray for purity — not just in body, but in motive.

I pray for clarity — not just in signs, but in peace.

If he's learning how to lead, give him grace to grow.

If he's unsure, don't let confusion speak louder than conviction.

And if this is the beginning of forever let it be built on You, brick by brick, prayer by prayer.

In Jesus' name, Amen.

PEACE IN THE PACE

Scripture Focus

"Do not arouse or awaken love until it so desires."

Song of Solomon 2:7 (NIV)

♫ Dedicated Song

"Fortunate" — Maxwell

This classic track speaks to the deep *gratitude and awe* of reconnecting with someone who feels like a gift from God.

Reflection

When God writes the story, there's no need to force the narrative.

Real love doesn't rush — it rests. Not in complacency, but in clarity. In this season, you weren't chasing butterflies or emotional highs. You were listening for God's voice. And in Hope, you didn't just find chemistry — you found confirmation.

God's timing is perfect. His peace becomes the pace. When both hearts are aligned with heaven, things begin to flow — not perfectly, but purposefully.

Your connection wasn't built on fantasy. It was built on friendship, faith, and the fruit of obedience. That's what made it sacred. And that's what made it sustainable.

Reflection Questions

1. What was different about the peace you felt in this relationship compared to others?

2. How can you tell when love is God-led versus emotionally driven?

3. In what ways did your relationship reflect friendship, not just romance?

4. Did you ever feel the urge to rush things — and how did you resist that?

5. How did your spiritual alignment affirm the pace and purpose of your relationship?

Prayer

Lord, thank You for divine alignment. Teach me to recognize the difference between emotion and Your voice. Help me to trust the pace You set and not rush ahead of Your will. Build relationships in my life that honor You from the ground up. In Jesus' name, Amen.

CHAPTER 6

GROWING LOVE

(FALL 2019)

Two are better than one, because they have a good
return for their labor:
If either of them falls down, one can help the other
up.
But pity anyone who falls and has no one to help
them up.
A cord of three strands is not quickly broken.

Ecclesiastes 4:9–12 (NIV)

The night air was cool enough to make her lean just a little closer as we walked side by side on base, the faint hum of the streetlights above us mixing with the steady rhythm of our footsteps. I remember catching the quiet curve of her smile in the corner of my eye, the kind that didn't need words because it was already saying, *I'm home here.*

Some verses don't just speak — they echo. This one was ours. Hope and I didn't just fall into love — we grew into it. Slowly, deliberately. The kind of love that isn't driven by fantasy but formed in the trenches of faith, intentionality, and time. What we were building was more than chemistry — it was covenant. And it showed up in the way we showed up for each other.

Everyday moments became sacred in her presence. Whether we were walking side by side on base, cooking dinner, or simply riding with the windows down and the music low, there was a rhythm to our love — unforced, but undeniable. It wasn't loud, but it was clear. It wasn't rushed, but it was real.

What made it different wasn't just how we loved — it was how we listened. Hope had a way of leaning in, not just with her ears, but with her heart. When I spoke, she didn't interrupt, fix, or deflect. She received. Her attention told me I mattered — not just as a man but as a story still being written. She didn't fall in love with who I was pretending to be. She saw the man in process and still chose me, again and again.

Her presence reminded me that love wasn't about performance — it was about peace. I had never known that kind of safety. With her, I didn't have to earn rest. I could just be. And in return, I wanted to protect what we had with the same intentionality she brought into every moment. Her tenderness sharpened me. Her faith inspired me. Her standards didn't intimidate me — they awakened something sacred within me: the desire to rise.

There was a moment I'll never forget. The late afternoon sun was melting into a golden haze, and the air carried that faint smell of gasoline and asphalt after a warm day. As we walked through the grocery store parking lot, our fingers interlaced, the world seemed muted except for the soft shuffle of our footsteps and the distant hum of car engines. We were walking through a grocery store parking lot, just holding hands, unaware of anything but each other, when I noticed a little girl staring at us from the backseat of a parked car. She couldn't have been more than ten, but her eyes were wide with quiet wonder. She wasn't smiling. She wasn't frowning. She was just watching — almost like she was seeing something she didn't know she needed.

Her face pressed lightly against the window, leaving a small oval of fog where her breath touched the glass. The reflection of the setting sun caught in her eyes, making them glimmer — not in joy exactly, but in a kind of longing that felt older than she was. It stopped me in my tracks internally, even as we kept walking.

That image lingered with me long after. It was a divine reminder that love doesn't just bless the ones inside of it — it bears witness to everyone around. If a child could recognize the beauty of what we shared, then surely God was using our love to plant seeds in places we couldn't even see. Our relationship wasn't just ours — it was a visible testimony. And in that moment, I realized something vital: real love doesn't have to be loud to be powerful. It just needs to be real.

But real love also requires real growth. And growth never happens without pruning.

Hope carried herself with a grace that was never arrogant but always assured. She knew who she was, and she knew what she deserved — not from entitlement, but from knowing her worth in God. She had standards that didn't bend to culture. She believed in honor, and she expected it. I learned this quickly. If I forgot to open her door, she would simply wait in the car. Not out of stubbornness — but out of principle.

At first, I didn't get it. I thought it was a small thing, a formality. But God used it to teach me something deeper. It wasn't about the door — it was about reverence. She was a daughter of the King, and she carried herself like it. Loving her meant recognizing her value — not just with words, but with actions. What felt like correction at first became my joy. Opening her door wasn't a chore — it was a declaration. A way to say, *I see you. I honor you. I choose to serve you — every day.*

In her presence, I learned that honor isn't about occasional gestures — it's about consistency. It's not in the grand moments. It's in the quiet ones. The way you speak to her when no one is listening. The way you protect her peace when your pride wants to win. The way you choose humility when it's easier to withdraw. Real honor flows from the recognition that love isn't just about what you feel — it's about what you build.

I remember a day on base when we were sitting in the car near the golf course. It was early evening, and the fading light washed the grass in soft amber tones. A light breeze carried the faint scent of freshly cut fairways, mingled with the distant clink of golf clubs being loaded into a bag. From where we sat, we could hear the muffled laughter of a group finishing their round. An older couple walked by, clearly finishing up their game, moving slowly but hand-in-hand. Their shoes made a gentle crunch against the gravel path, and I remember how the woman's white visor cast a shadow over her face as she glanced up at the man beside her. I smiled and said, "That's going to be us in 40 years." But Hope shook her head gently and said, "No, it's not." At first, I was confused. Then she explained, "He didn't open her door."

That moment marked me. It wasn't about criticizing the man. It was about protecting the standard. Love doesn't grow old — it just changes form. But honor? That should never fade. What you do in the beginning should still matter decades later. She didn't want seasonal affection — she wanted eternal consistency. And that conviction made me want to be better — not just for her, but for God.

Brother to Brother

They're watching how you love. How you show up. How you lead — not just in public but in private. Your relationship isn't just about romance — it's a sermon. If God is truly at the center, your love should preach even when you're silent. The way you pray together, forgive one another, navigate disappointment, and celebrate the mundane — it all tells a story. Not of perfection, but of redemption.

This generation doesn't need more relationship goals. It needs more godly examples. And that starts with us.

You don't have to be flawless. You just have to be faithful. Keep God at the center — because a cord of three strands isn't easily broken. And when He is the foundation, love doesn't just survive — it thrives. It grows through winter. It anchors through storms. It endures through silence. God doesn't just strengthen your love — He sanctifies it. He sets it apart for His glory.

So don't just invite Him in — build around Him. Let Him define your rhythm. Let Him interrupt your plans. Let Him refine your posture. Because when God knits two hearts together, it's never just about them — it's about legacy.

That little girl in the backseat? She may never remember our faces. But maybe she walked away believing love like ours was still possible. That's the power of a relationship rooted in heaven. It doesn't just touch your life — it plants seeds in others.

This isn't just about being in love. It's about being in covenant. And covenant love doesn't just feel good — it bears fruit. It heals. It protects. It endures. And it points back to the One who authored it in the first place.

Brother to Sister: Pray for His Growth and Honor

Sis, falling in love is easy, but growing in love takes work. It takes pruning. It takes patience. It takes presence. And while he may not always say it, the weight of becoming a godly man who honors you while still becoming himself is real.

So don't just pray for butterflies. Pray for depth.

Pray that his love won't just impress you — it'll cover you, protect you, and reflect God's heart. Because true love doesn't just flirt. It builds. Honors. Waits. And the man who loves you well will first be a man who lets God grow him through the uncomfortable moments.

Pray this over him:

Lord, I pray for the man who's learning how to love, not just with words, but with action, honor, and humility.

Teach him to love me like You've loved him — without pressure, without pretense.

Grow his capacity to lead with tenderness.

Stretch his understanding of what it means to serve.

In the moments where his growth feels slow, give me patience.

In the moments where pruning is painful, give him strength.

Don't let public affirmation mean more to him than private obedience.

Keep his love rooted in You, not in performance.

And when the world tries to define what love looks like —

Let him mirror the quiet, unshakable kind that heaven recognizes.

In Jesus' name, Amen.

ROOTED IN SOMETHING REAL

Scripture Focus

> *"So then, just as you received Christ Jesus as Lord,
> continue to live your lives in Him, rooted and built
> up in Him, strengthened in the faith as you were
> taught, and overflowing with thankfulness."*
>
> **Colossians 2:6–7 (NIV)**

♫ **Dedicated Song**

"Promise" — Ciara

This song captures the essence of a love that is intentional, devoted, and divinely inspired.

Reflection

Real love doesn't just feel good — it bears fruit.

In this season, your relationship wasn't built on superficial attraction. It was built on spiritual alignment. Her prayers matched yours. Her vision complemented yours. Her presence pushed you toward purpose. That's what made it sacred.

The most powerful love stories are the ones where God is not an accessory — He's the anchor.

Your growth didn't come from perfect days. It came from intentional moments. Conversations that healed. Honesty that

sharpened. Forgiveness that softened. You were building something eternal, not just emotional.

Reflection Questions

1. What spiritual disciplines helped nurture your relationship during this season?

2. How did your partner's faith and honesty challenge you
   to grow personally?

3. In what ways did emotional safety contribute to deeper
   spiritual intimacy?

4. Were there any areas where you saw God stretching your
   love to become more selfless?

5. What fruit from this season still shows up in your life
   today?

Prayer

*Father, thank You for teaching me that love grows
best when it's rooted in You. Help me to love with
intention, humility, and grace. May my relationships reflect heaven — not just in moments, but in
foundation. In Jesus' name, Amen.*

PART THREE

THE JOURNEY TO "I DO"

(2020–2023)

CHAPTER 7

THE COVID SEASON

"He who finds a wife finds what is good and receives favor from the Lord."

Proverbs 18:22 (NIV)

T his verse became more than just scripture to me — it became my compass. Some moments aren't just memories — they're the place where love stops being a feeling and becomes a vow.

From the moment I found Hope, I recognized something sacred in her. She wasn't just a beautiful woman with a kind spirit — she was a gift. A living, breathing promise. I knew it in my spirit. I didn't need a ceremony or a legal document to begin treating her like the woman God had set apart for me. Long before I ever dropped to one knee, I made a private covenant in my heart: I would love her like a husband should. I would honor her, cover her, and create a space where she felt safe, seen, and secure.

And then, just as our relationship was finding its rhythm, the world came to a halt.

In early 2020, COVID-19 disrupted life as we knew it. The pace of the world slowed, but the noise in people's minds grew louder — fear, loss, uncertainty. What used to be routine — gatherings, dinners out, hugs, handshakes — suddenly became restricted, even dangerous. But in the middle of global chaos, something beautiful was quietly being built between us. While so many were unraveling, Hope and I found an unusual peace. It was as if God had pulled us aside to whisper, *Focus on each other. Build this. Protect this.*

With the world on pause, distractions faded. There were no busy schedules, no conflicting plans, no external pressures. It was just us. And in that stillness, we grew. I wasn't working during that time, and Hope, being a full-time real estate agent, had flexibility that allowed us to spend intentional time together. While shelves in stores emptied and the world scrambled, we had access to the military base. The BX and commissary became our refuge, a place where we could find what we needed — sometimes rationed, sometimes scarce — but enough.

I took it as my responsibility, and my privilege, to make sure she and her mother never lacked. Every grocery run became an act of covering. I wasn't just buying food — I was providing peace. I stocked up on paper towels, cleaning supplies, toiletries, water — anything they might need. Not out of fear, but out of love. Out of the conviction that this was what love looked like: preparation, protection, and provision. I didn't want Hope to worry about anything. She had been strong for so long. Now it was my turn to carry the weight.

And while we were meeting needs on the outside, something even deeper was happening on the inside. We were learning each other in a way most couples never get the chance to. We talked. I mean really talked — about our pasts, our traumas, our dreams, our fears. There was no makeup, no distractions, no hiding. Just truth. And through it all, I came to know her not just as a woman I loved, but as a woman I respected, trusted, and admired.

Hope is naturally reserved — quiet and cautious. But with me, she slowly began to open. I cherished those moments, the ones where her guard dropped and her voice softened. One night, she said something that branded my heart forever: "If you ever feel like you need to be with someone else, let me know, because I can make another choice." That one sentence carried the weight of trust and boundaries. It wasn't a threat — it was a sacred boundary. She wasn't going to beg to be chosen. She knew her worth. And in that moment, I made a decision I've never regretted: I would never make her question whether she was enough.

Even before I asked her to be my wife, I treated her as though she already was. The way I prayed for her. The way I protected her. The way I held space for her to be fully herself. I wasn't waiting for a ring to give her my loyalty — I gave it freely, because I knew. In my heart, I was already hers. I was just waiting for her to catch up.

When her birthday approached in the fall, I wanted to do something unforgettable. Something worthy of her. She was turning 49, and deep down, I sensed that this birthday marked more than just another year — it felt like a prophetic threshold. In my spirit, I knew that by the time she turned 50, something would have shifted. We would no longer be preparing — we would be walking in what God had called us to.

So, I planned a surprise birthday celebration that would reflect the depth of my love and the honor she deserved. I chose 12 Stories in D.C., a rooftop lounge that carried the kind of elegance and excellence that matched her spirit. I didn't want a generic party — I wanted a moment. A memory. An altar.

I reached out to her friends. Her mother. Even her father, who lived in Florida. I knew how much it would mean for him to be there. I'll never forget the feeling when he said yes. His presence alone was the gift I prayed for her to receive. The only challenge left was getting her there without suspicion.

That day, I stalled her in the parking garage, pretending to be on a phone call about someone needing to send me money. She grew frustrated, visibly annoyed — but even then, she was patient. She had no idea what waited just one elevator ride away. When the moment was right, I led her upstairs to the VIP section. At first, she was still tense — until she saw them. Her mother.

Her father. Her closest friends. The look on her face — shock, then joy, then deep gratitude — made every sacrifice worth it.

Her father looked at me, smiled, and said, "You really got her." That one sentence held a father's approval, a silent blessing.

That night was magical. Not because I had money to spend — I didn't. I sacrificed to make it happen. But that's what love does. It gives. It shows up. It doesn't calculate worth based on budget — it pours out what's priceless. She danced with her mother. Laughed with her friends. Swung gently in her father's arms. Hope has videos from that night — videos that still make her smile. Videos that captured more than a party. They captured joy. Belonging. And love that had been earned through consistency.

Later, she asked if anyone helped pay for the celebration. I told her no. Not because I was proud, but because I wanted it to be a pure gift. No strings. No expectations. Just honor. Because love that is pure gives without keeping score. I always will believe that you can't put a price tag on memories.

That night wasn't just a birthday. It was a declaration: I see you. I choose you. I'm committed to loving you with everything I have.

As the months passed and the world adjusted to a new normal, I felt the tug in my spirit — it was time. The time to move from covenant in my heart to covenant in the open. I wanted to propose. But first, I did what I believe every man should do: I sought her parents' blessing. Her mother gave hers with a full heart. Her father, over the phone, said simply, "Take care of my daughter." And I promised that I would.

I had a custom suit made — something I rarely do. But this wasn't just another night. It was sacred. I made reservations at La Vie, an elegant waterfront restaurant in D.C. The kind of place where love could be sealed with beauty and reverence. I even hired a driver and asked two close friends — from her circle and one from mine — to be there, quietly witnessing it all.

She didn't know. She just knew this night felt different.

As we pulled up to the restaurant, she smiled, curious but content. We sat at a private table overlooking the water. The sun was setting. There was peace in the air. Everything was perfect. We shared a lavish seafood platter and leaned into each other's presence. At one point, we took a photo — just the two of us, beaming. That photo now hangs in my home, frozen in time, a snapshot of destiny unfolding.

After dinner, we stepped outside. The driver waited nearby. The ring burned in my pocket — a ring I had admired for three years, praying one day I'd be able to give it to her. We drove to Turner Cliffs — the very place where we had first reconnected. It wasn't just a spot on the map — it was sacred ground. And now, it would be the place where I would ask her to become my wife.

She saw our friends standing nearby with their phones. Confused, she looked at me.

I took her hand. Walked her forward. Then I stopped. Looked into her eyes. And told her everything my heart had been holding.

Then I knelt.

"Will you marry me?"

She stared at me in silence, looking shocked.

"Are you serious?" she whispered.

"Yes," I said.

And in that sacred pause between question and answer, the world seemed to hush.

She said yes.

Cheers erupted — not just from our friends but from strangers nearby, their clapping mixing with the soft rustle of the warm wind through the trees. In that moment, even the fading light seemed to lean in, wrapping us in a warm, golden glow as her hand slid into mine. When our masks came off and our lips met, I could taste the lingering sweetness of the evening air. It wasn't just a kiss. It was covenant. It was joy. It was heaven smiling on earth.

The crowd around us — strangers at nearby restaurants — began to clap. Cheer. Celebrate.

We drove away in silence, understanding the weight in that moment with hearts overflowing. That night wasn't just a proposal — it was the beginning of a promise. A divine yes that echoed into eternity.

Brother to Brother: Walking in Faith

Brother, when you know God's hand is on something — don't hesitate. Don't overthink it. Don't wait for a sign in the sky or the approval of people who were never called to carry your assignment. When the peace of God confirms what your spirit already knows, that's your green light. Walk in it. Boldly. Completely. Without apology. Because what God calls you into, He has already gone ahead of you to prepare.

Not everything that's divine will feel easy. In fact, the moment you step toward what's sacred, you can expect resistance. The enemy doesn't fight what isn't a threat. And sometimes, that resistance won't come in the form of storms or strangers — but through the subtle, well-meaning voices of people you love. Friends. Family. Even spiritual leaders. They may speak words wrapped in concern, but laced with fear. They may caution you, not because they don't believe in you, but because they're still healing from battles they lost or prayers that went unanswered.

You must discern the difference between wisdom and worry. Between God's voice and good intentions.

Not every opinion is ordained. Not every concern is confirmation. And not every hesitation you feel is a *no* — sometimes, it's just the weight of stepping into something holy.

This is why your relationship with God must be rooted, not rented. You can't borrow conviction. You can't live off someone else's revelation. You need to know God's voice for yourself. You need to recognize His presence in the quiet and His direction in the stillness. When He speaks — move. When He confirms — don't delay. When He calls you into covenant — honor it with everything you are.

There will be moments when it feels too big for you. Moments when doubt creeps in and logic tries to override faith. But Brother, faith was never about what made sense — it was always about what made surrender. God never asked you to understand every detail. He asked you to trust Him with the outcome.

If He gave you the assignment, He will give you the grace to carry it.

So, guard your peace. Protect your circle. Listen to wisdom but follow the whisper of the Spirit above all else. Because when God is in it — no man, no critic, no fear, and no weapon formed against it will prosper.

Walk in faith, even if your knees are trembling.

Walk in love, even when it costs you something.

Walk in purpose, even when the path is unfamiliar.

And remember this truth deep in your bones: when God joins two lives together, it is not a suggestion — it is a declaration. Heaven has spoken. Let no man, no insecurity, and no moment of weakness separate what God Himself has set in motion.

You don't have to force what God has favored. You just have to follow His lead.

Brother to Sister:
Pray for His Endurance in the Unknown

Sis, there are seasons when the world stops, but growth doesn't. When plans fall apart, but purpose is still unfolding. And for a man trying to lead, love, and stay grounded in uncertainty, it can be a quiet battle.

He may not show the fear. He may not express the pressure. But deep down, he's asking, *How do I stay steady when everything feels unstable?*

That's where your prayers carry weight.

Don't just pray for good times. Pray that he learns to hold fast when nothing is certain — to love well when everything else is unclear. Because a man who learns to endure in the unknown is a man who will lead with peace, not panic.

Pray this over him:

Lord, I pray for the man who's walking through a season of uncertainty.

Remind him that he's not alone.

Show him that stability doesn't come from perfect plans — but from Your presence.

When he feels helpless, be his anchor.

When he feels the pressure to perform, let him rest in grace.

Strengthen his faith in the silence.

Deepen his trust in the pause.

Teach him how to love from the inside out.

Not through grand gestures, but through quiet consistency.

And if this season is stretching him, don't let him break.

Let him bend toward You.

In Jesus' name, Amen.

CHOOSING COVENANT OVER CULTURE

Scripture Focus

> *"He who finds a wife finds what is good and receives favor from the Lord."*
>
> **Proverbs 18:22 (NIV)**

♫ Dedicated Song

"All of Me" — John Legend

A heartfelt love ballad that celebrates full commitment and vulnerability — perfect for the weight and joy of engagement.

Reflection

In a world that glorifies proposals for the pictures, God calls you to prepare for the promise.

The question wasn't just *Will she say yes?* It was *God, is this who You've set apart for me?* You weren't chasing romance — you were responding to revelation. This wasn't about impressing her with a ring; it was about inviting her into a covenant that would be tested, refined, and anointed.

Marriage isn't just a partnership — it's a spiritual assignment. And when you asked, you weren't just asking her hand — you were inviting her heart to walk with yours under the authority of Christ.

This sacred *yes* wasn't just hers — it was yours, too. To honor. To lead. To protect. To serve.

Reflection Questions

1. What did your engagement reveal about your readiness — spiritually, emotionally, and relationally?

2. How did God confirm the timing and the covenant before you proposed?

3. In what ways did culture pressure you to perform instead of preparing your heart?

4. What responsibilities did you feel God calling you to carry as a future husband?

5. How did you seek counsel or cover before saying yes to forever?

Prayer

Lord, thank You for the gift of confirmation. Help me to honor covenant more than culture. Give me the wisdom to propose not just with love, but with intention. Prepare my heart to lead, serve, and protect according to Your will. In Jesus' name, Amen.

CHAPTER 8

OUR WEDDING
AND HONEYMOON STORY

*"And over all these virtues put on love, which binds
them all together in perfect unity."*

Colossians 3:14 (NIV)

This scripture isn't just a beautiful verse to read at weddings — it is a divine reminder that love must lead. Before the vows, the rings, the music, and the celebration — there must be understanding, sacrifice, and spiritual preparation. Love that is not anchored in preparation can feel magical in the moment but crumble under the weight of reality. The scripture calls us beyond the celebration into the sober, steady work of building a covenant that can weather storms.

Hope and I both knew that love alone, though essential, wasn't enough. We needed wisdom. We needed counsel. And we needed to face truth — about ourselves, about each other, and about what it truly means to walk together in covenant.

We chose to participate in premarital counseling through two sources. First, a trusted deacon from our church who helped us understand marriage from a biblical lens. With grace and candor, he guided us through the spiritual weight of vows — how marriage isn't just a legal contract, but a divine covenant. Love that is not anchored in preparation can feel magical in the moment but crumble under the weight of reality. The scripture calls us beyond the celebration into the sober, steady work of building a covenant that can weather storms. We also sought the help of a professional counselor, someone neutral, who challenged us to unpack our personal histories, values, and fears.

One of the most important revelations during this process came as we discussed our backgrounds. Hope was used to being the decision-maker, forging ahead with confidence and self-reliance. She had been an only child, and although previously married, she had no children of her own. I, on the other hand, had been married and had a daughter as well as a step-son. The different past lessons, responsibilities, and adjustments in our lives informed our perspectives on what it meant to live with another person.

Counseling exposed the areas where our stories collided — and where they complemented each other. It showed us the beauty of alignment, but also the necessity of surrender. It taught us that in order to truly become one, we had to let go of the need to always be right and instead embrace the need to always be real. Oneness was not going to happen by accident — it had to be chosen, protected, and fought for long before the first disagreement ever came.

No subject was off-limits. Finances, intimacy, expectations, parenting, communication styles — even fears of failure. Nothing was too sacred to be addressed. We learned that hiding things before marriage only sets the stage for conflict after. Honesty, though sometimes uncomfortable, was the doorway to trust.

Marriage counseling didn't just prepare us for the wedding — it prepared us for life.

The Wedding Journey: Anticipation and Execution

Throughout my life, I had attended many weddings. I had watched grooms hold their breath as the music changed. I had seen tears in their eyes, nervous hands clutching bouquets or wiping sweat from their brows. But I always paid attention to one thing: the moment the groom sees his bride.

Because in that moment, everything else fades. It's just him and her. And everything becomes still. The world blurs, the noise drops away, and time slows to the speed of love.

Hope and I came into our wedding journey with two very different pasts. My first marriage had been a quiet, low-key courthouse ceremony — short, simple, and without the fanfare. Hope, on the other hand, had already experienced a beautiful, traditional wedding. So when the time came to plan ours, she initially insisted that we didn't need anything extravagant.

But in my heart, I longed for a different kind of experience — something sacred, something public, something holy. I wanted to see my bride walk down the aisle. I wanted a memory I could hold onto forever.

She graciously gave me the reins. "Plan what you want," she said. "Whatever you envision — I'll show up."

So, I got to work. I found a beautiful golf course that overlooked the water — a peaceful, elegant setting that mirrored the kind of atmosphere I hoped would reflect our love. I booked it nearly a year in advance, wanting everything to be just right.

Planning a wedding was more intense than I expected. Thankfully, I had a few women in our lives who stepped in to help with details that, truthfully, I would have missed. From the floral arrangements to the music to the colors Hope would love, they made sure nothing was overlooked. I handled the big pieces — the catering, the limo, the tuxedo fittings. But they handled the heart. Their touches turned my plans into something living, breathing, and unforgettable.

With each passing week, anticipation grew. This wasn't just an event — it was a sacred shift in our lives.

The Ceremony: A Moment to Remember

We decided to have two ceremonies. The first was a small, intimate church wedding on Friday, November 3, 2023. Just the two of us, the pastor, and God. It was quiet, reverent, and deeply meaningful. In that still sanctuary, it felt like heaven leaned close to listen. There's something powerful about exchanging vows in a sanctuary — just you, your covenant, and the One who holds it all together.

The second ceremony took place on November 4 at the golf course, surrounded by family and friends. The air was electric with joy. As the music began and guests stood, I looked down the aisle — first came Hope's mother, walking as our flower girl, followed by her cousin as a bridesmaid. Then … I saw her.

Hope.

Even though I had just seen her in her dress the night before, something about this moment undid me. She was radiant — glowing, poised, breathtaking. I had to fight back tears. Actually, I failed to fight them. They fell freely.

It wasn't just how she looked — it was what she represented. A second chance. A divine restoration. A covenant renewed.

When we exchanged vows, I held onto every word. But there was one thing she said that gripped me and still echoes in my soul:

"I can't wait to see what God has called you to do in life, and I will always be a safe place for you to land."

Those words became a covering. A reminder that I didn't just have a wife — I had a partner, a refuge, a believer in my purpose.

At that altar, I felt heaven's affirmation: This is the one.

After the ceremony, we entered into celebration. The reception was alive with music, laughter, and love. People danced, ate, shared stories, and filled the room with warmth.

Our first dance was like a scene from a movie, one I never wanted to end. Every detail had fallen into place. But more than that, our hearts were aligned. The joy in the room wasn't just about décor or entertainment. It was the presence of God. It was the presence of peace.

And as the night closed, we returned to our hotel, hand in hand, now husband and wife — ready for the next chapter.

The Honeymoon: A Journey of Love and Dependence

Because I had taken the lead in planning the wedding, Hope took responsibility for the honeymoon — and she didn't disappoint.

She planned a dream trip to Thailand — somewhere neither of us had ever been. We flew from Dulles to Seoul, South Korea (a 15.5-hour flight), followed by another five-hour flight to Bangkok. It was exhausting, but unforgettable. Every hour in the air felt like a countdown to an adventure we would never forget.

Our suite on the 24th floor of the Atheny Hotel was exquisite. Floor-to-ceiling windows, separate lounge areas, and a breakfast buffet that overlooked the entire city — it felt like a dream.

We explored local markets, tasted authentic Thai cuisine, and were welcomed with kindness and respect by everyone we met. Their humility and warmth made us feel at home.

One evening, we visited the highest rooftop bar in Thailand — on the 52nd floor, with sweeping views of the city. When they found out we were on our honeymoon, they surprised us with dessert and live music. It was magical.

After a few days in Bangkok, we traveled to the Phi Phi Islands — arguably one of the most beautiful places on earth.

The one-hour speedboat ride across turquoise waters brought us to a paradise I didn't know existed. We swam in 86-degree water, explored seafood markets, and soaked in the beauty of the islands.

Our resort had an infinity pool that became our secret hideaway. And on our final days, we stayed in a private villa with its own pool — secluded, quiet, and perfect.

One night, while lying in the bed I looked at Hope and said, "I still have butterflies being here with you." She smiled and asked if I was just now getting them?

I told her the truth: "It's not the place. It's the way we had to fully depend on each other while being on the other side of the world. That's what gives me butterflies."

That's what marriage is. Not just romance — but reliance. Not just excitement — but interdependence. It's knowing that no matter where you are in the world, the one beside you is home.

Ten days later, we returned to the U.S., exhausted but full. The jet lag hit hard — but so did reality. The wedding was over.

The honeymoon had ended. But our life together? That was just the beginning.

We quickly realized that marriage doesn't end at "I do." It starts there. Everything else is the daily choice to love, forgive, grow, and serve.

We entered this next chapter with faith, unity, and the promise that we'd walk it out together — hand in hand, heart to heart.

Brother to Brother: Walking in Faith

Brother, when you know God's hand is on something, don't tiptoe into it — walk boldly. Step like you've been sent. Move like you've been marked. This isn't the time to second-guess what heaven has already confirmed. If the Spirit whispered it, that whisper is enough. You don't need the approval of a crowd when you've been anointed in secret.

There will be distractions. There will be delays. There will be moments that make you question what you heard. But don't confuse resistance with misdirection. Just because it's hard doesn't mean it's wrong. Some of the clearest calls from God are followed by the loudest chaos. And sometimes, the very opposition you face is the proof that you're walking in divine order.

Here's what you have to remember: not every voice that speaks into your life is sent by God. Be careful who you let counsel your calling. Some warnings come wrapped in fear. Some advice comes tainted by past pain. Even well-meaning voices can plant seeds of doubt that have nothing to do with wisdom and everything to do with wounds. And if you're not careful, you'll abort something God is birthing in you because someone else couldn't see it growing.

You've got to guard your inner circle with the same intensity that you guard your purpose. This walk isn't for applause. It's not for validation. It's not for those who only show up when they understand. This is for the man who knows that when God says move, you move — even if your feet are trembling.

And don't let your own doubts disqualify you. Don't talk yourself out of what God has already equipped you for. You may not feel ready. You may not have every detail. But God doesn't ask for your perfection — He asks for your obedience. And sometimes, the greatest leap of faith isn't into a pulpit or a spotlight — it's into a moment that no one sees but heaven.

So, walk with your head high and your spirit grounded. Walk like a man who knows who called him. Walk like someone who understands that the path may twist, but the promise doesn't change. There's a purpose on your life that hell can't cancel, and every step you take in faith is a step closer to the fulfillment of that promise.

You're not crazy for believing. You're not weak for hoping. You're not naïve for trusting again. You're just a man who knows that if God started it, He's going to finish it.

So, take the step. Send the message. Show up. Speak life. Build anyway. Love anyway. Forgive anyway. Walk anyway.

Because when you walk in faith, you don't just shift your circumstances — you shift the atmosphere around you.

This is more than a decision. It's a declaration. You believe God.

And that belief will move mountains — starting with the ones inside of you. And when you walk like that, Brother — love doesn't just find you, it follows you.

Brother to Sister: Pray for His Covenant Heart

Sis, every man who gets down on one knee is stepping into more than a moment — he's stepping into mission. Engagement isn't just excitement — it's weight. It's spiritual warfare. It's the beginning of a promise that the enemy will try to distract, delay, or destroy.

Your prayers, right now, matter more than ever.

Don't just pray for a beautiful wedding. Pray for a man whose *yes* is rooted in obedience. A man who chooses covenant over convenience. A man who hears from God and follows through — even when it costs him comfort.

Pray this over him:

Lord, I pray for the man who has said yes — not just to me, but to You.

Make his yes sacred.

Make it sober.

Make it strong.

Strip away anything in him that confuses love with control.

Remove fear, pride, or hesitation masked as preparation.

Teach him how to fight in the Spirit.

Teach him how to lead with humility.

Let every detail of our engagement be more than planning — let it be preparation.

Preparation for purpose.

Preparation for war.

Preparation for love that reflects Your glory.

I don't need perfection from him.

I just need presence.

And I trust that You're shaping him to be a husband not just in title, but in spirit.

In Jesus' name, Amen.

MORE THAN A MOMENT

Scripture Focus

"Therefore what God has joined together, let no one separate."

Mark 10:9 (NIV)

♫ Dedicated Song

"When I Say I Do" — Matthew West

This song captures the sacred weight of saying "I do" before God, and the daily grace it takes to live those words out in love.

Reflection

The wedding day is a celebration, but the covenant is a calling.

While others saw flowers, music, and elegant attire — you saw the altar. You saw the weight of your yes. You saw your bride not just as the woman you loved, but as the partner God had chosen for your purpose.

This wasn't about a beautiful day. It was about a lifelong promise.

The wedding journey wasn't perfect—but it was holy. God used every detail — the counseling, the obstacles, the intimacy of prayer — to purify your hearts and anchor your intentions. Your yes wasn't casual. It was sacred. Not just to her, but to Him.

Reflection Questions

1. What fears or doubts did you have leading up to the wedding, and how did you confront them spiritually?

2. How did God speak to you during the preparation process — not just for the day, but for the covenant?

3. What did you learn about unity, sacrifice, or selflessness through wedding counseling or planning?

4. What did the ceremony represent to you beyond the celebration?

5. How do you plan to keep the vow sacred when the emotions wear off?

Prayer

Father, thank You for covenant. Thank You for showing me that marriage is more than a moment — it's a mission. Help me never lose sight of the sacredness of my yes. Let my love be a reflection of Your love, today and always. In Jesus' name, Amen.

PART FOUR

WHEN WORLDS COLLIDE

(2024)

CHAPTER 9

MOVING IN

"Be completely humble and gentle; be patient, bear-
ing with one another in love. Make every effort to
keep the unity of the Spirit through the bond of peace."

Ephesians 4:2–3 (NIV)

L ove isn't just a feeling — it's a decision you have to wake
up and make again and again. It's not just candlelit dinners or whispered prayers before bed. It's the patient
inhale when she does things differently than you. The grace to
bite your tongue when you're tempted to defend your "way." It's
humility when your ego rises, gentleness when your pride says
"prove a point."

Real love is forged in the fire of proximity — when you're
not just dating her, you're doing life with her. The way the light
spills across the kitchen table in the morning, catching the steam
from her coffee, becomes just as much a part of love as the quiet
"goodnight" at the end of the day. And nothing will test your

understanding of love like sharing a living space with the one you've prayed for.

We did the work — we prayed, counseled, planned. But no plan can fully prepare your heart for the sacred disruption that comes when two worlds collide under one roof. Marriage counseling gives you tools. But living together gives you tests. And those tests reveal what the tools can't teach. They expose how deep your surrender really goes.

For years, I lived alone. My apartment was mine — simple, peaceful, unbothered. It knew my rhythm, my mess, my prayers, my pain. Onyx — my faithful companion — held my secrets. He watched me cry, heal, and grow. That space held me through silence and sorrow. There was no one to adjust for, no one to explain to. Just peace in the solitude. But whenever Hope came over — everything shifted.

I'd find myself sweeping floors that hadn't seen a broom in days, breathing in the citrus tang of freshly sprayed cleaner, lighting candles I didn't even like, watching the soft flicker dance against the walls, tidying corners I used to overlook. Not out of performance, but out of honor.

I wanted her to feel something when she walked in. Not just comfort. Value. Respect. Belonging. She always knew, though. Every time she'd smile and tease, "Did the people come?" referring to a cleaning service I obviously would use. It became our inside joke. She saw the effort, not the flaws. She wasn't judging — she was loving. She didn't need perfection — she just wanted presence.

I wasn't cleaning because I was pretending. I was preparing. Preparing for what life might be like when it was no longer just me. But no matter how much you prepare, visits are not reality. You can clean for company, but you can't hide when you live together — not for long.

The day I moved into Hope's home wasn't just a day of excitement — it was a day of reckoning. I carried my boxes and my baggage. I brought my clothes, my habits, my assumptions, my way of doing things. And so did she. Two stories converging in one space. Two patterns now overlapping. Two lives becoming one.

Suddenly the bed wasn't just mine. The toothpaste, the thermostat, the coffee schedule — all shared. And even Onyx had to adjust. Hope had a rule: no dogs upstairs. That rule stung more than I expected, because Onyx wasn't just a dog. He was a thread of loyalty, my emotional anchor. At night, I missed the soft sound of his paws on the floor and the way he'd sigh before curling up beside me. But this wasn't just my space anymore. It was ours. And love means honoring what makes her feel safe, even when it stretches what makes you feel at home.

Then the small things started speaking loudly. The way I folded towels — wrong. The way I washed the dishes — disorganized. The closet — don't even talk about the closet. Her side smelled faintly of fresh linen; my side still carried the scent of cedar from my old apartment. Hope had created an atmosphere of structure. Not out of control, but out of necessity. Out of survival. Out of the need to feel peace in her home.

She never made me feel unwelcome. But there were moments I felt like a visitor. Like I had to ask permission to breathe. Like I was watching a dance I didn't know the steps to. Her rhythm had a sound — coffee aroma in the early morning, water running for tea at night, the quiet shuffle of her slippers across the hardwood floor. She had a rhythm — and I was still finding my footing. And I didn't want to just blend into her world. I wanted to build something new.

One night, I tried to say what I couldn't quite name. The kitchen was dim except for the amber glow of the pendant light over the island, casting long shadows on the counter. "If you're at a ten and I'm at a two," I said, "I'm not ignoring it ... I'm just growing." She looked at me with honesty that cut past the surface. "I told you I'd give you time," she said. "But if I do, you'll turn my house into Tribeca." Tribeca was the name of my apartment that I moved from.

That hit harder than I expected. She wasn't just talking about routines. She was talking about fear — about losing the sanctuary she had built, about watching her peace get drowned out by my old patterns. And I got it. But I needed her to get me, too.

Marriage doesn't mean erasing who you are. It means becoming something new — together. It's not about one life folding into another. It's about both surrendering to God's design for something neither one of you could create alone.

That takes more than love. It takes humility — to admit you don't know everything. Grace — to give space for growing pains. Faith — to believe God's hand is steady, even when your steps are shaky. You don't just move into a home. You move into a process. And that process will sanctify you if you let it.

Because unity doesn't just happen. It's built. In the mundane. In the disagreements. In the clink of dishes being stacked away after dinner, in the hush of the house after a misunderstanding, in the golden light of late afternoon spilling across the living room as you sit together in silence. In the dishes and the silence and the subtle adjustments. In choosing peace over pettiness, love over control, surrender over stubbornness. You don't build a marriage with grand gestures. You build it with quiet obedience. With whispered prayers behind closed doors. With forgiveness when it's not deserved. With consistency when it's not convenient.

Moving in wasn't just a physical shift. It was spiritual. Emotional. Sacrificial. And every day, I had to ask myself — am I building a life, or just taking up space? Because the goal isn't to survive the merge. It's to become one through it. And that … that is a holy thing.

Brother to Brother:
This Ain't Just Her House — It's Your Calling

To the man who just moved in, or is about to take that step — to the one learning how to share not just a space, but a life — listen closely. This isn't just a change of address. It's a shift in your assignment. And if you're paying attention, God is using this very moment to do something deeper in you than comfort ever could.

Marriage doesn't just expose your habits — it exposes your heart. You can clean the place up, say the right prayers, even watch a dozen videos on how to fold towels and organize drawers. But there will come a moment when you realize this isn't just your apartment or your sanctuary anymore. This is no longer about "your way." It's "ours" now. And that word — ours — will stretch you in ways you didn't expect.

You're used to having your own rhythm. Your own setup. Your own logic that governs where things go and how things flow. You're used to walking in and knowing the environment bends to your preference. But when God brings two lives together, He's not just merging routines — He's merging destinies. And in that merger, comfort bows to calling.

You're not just stepping into a shared space. You're stepping into sacred ground. This isn't a domestic arrangement — it's a divine appointment. You're not just moving into a house — you're stepping into a refining fire. But hear me, brother: if God is in it, that fire won't destroy you — it will define you.

Because it takes a strong man to share space without losing self-control. It takes maturity to see correction not as criticism, but as a chance to grow. It takes security to admit that maybe her way is better, or at least different, and still worthy of honor. And it takes spiritual vision to see that God uses dishes, laundry, calendars, and conversations to do what altars and pulpits sometimes can't.

So let me speak life into you:

You're not weak because you're learning to adjust. You're wise.

You're not soft because you listen and respond with gentleness. You're strong enough to evolve.

You're not losing your identity. You're becoming the husband God had in mind when He created you.

I know the temptation. When you've lived on your own long enough, you build emotional muscle that can look like independence but is really self-preservation. You develop rituals that feel like peace but are actually fortresses. So, when you walk into a home that's no longer just yours, and you feel like a guest in your own space, it doesn't mean you're being pushed out. It means you're being invited in — invited to co-create something brand new, not drag in old patterns masked as "how I've always done it."

She doesn't need a version of you that has it all figured out. She just needs you — present, consistent, real. Not the version of yourself that hides behind ego or expects her to adapt to all your edges. She needs the man who's willing to smooth those edges with grace. She's not trying to erase you. She's trying to build with you. But she can't do that unless you show up fully — open hands, open heart, surrendered pride.

- So slow down and listen.
- Give her grace.
- Ask for patience when you miss it.
- Pray together — even when it feels awkward.
- Have the hard conversations. And then have them again.

Real men don't fight for control — they fight for connection. They don't dominate. They protect. They don't retreat when it gets uncomfortable — they lean in with courage.

You're not building a house of ease. You're building a sanctuary of covenant. A place where peace is cultivated, not just expected. A place where both of you can breathe and grow and stretch and forgive without fear of abandonment.

So, every time you wake up in that bed next to her, ask God, "How can I love better today than I did yesterday? How can I serve in a way that reflects Your love for the Church?"

Because in the end, it won't matter who folds the towels right.

What will matter is whether your love is folded in humility and laced with grace. Whether you create an atmosphere where she can rest and rise, weep and worship, correct and be covered.

This isn't just her house. It's your calling.

And if God trusted you with it, He expects you to build it — not like a tenant — but like a steward. Like a man who understands the weight of what he's been given and treats it as holy.

So, rise up, brother. This is more than a move-in. It's a move of God.

Brother to Sister: Pray for His Sensitivity to Your Space

Sis, he may be moving in — but you're the one giving up more than anyone realizes. Your routines, your sanctuary, your solitude — all of it's being stretched to make room for someone else. And even if he's kind … even if he's helpful … there's still a weight that comes with sharing your peace.

So, don't just pray for harmony. Pray for his sensitivity.

That he doesn't bulldoze his way in. That he doesn't mistake your silence for moodiness. That he sees your heart, not just your habits. Because real love doesn't just take up space — it learns how to honor it.

Pray this over him:

Lord, I pray for the man who's stepping into my world — my space, my rhythms, my life.

Help him not just to settle in, but to settle with care.

When I seem distant, let him lean in gently.

When I need quiet, let him not take it personally.

When I feel overwhelmed, let him respond with grace, not frustration.

Teach him to notice the little things —

The drawers I've always used, the way I like my mornings, the sanctuary I've built.

Let his presence be peace, not pressure.

Let his adjustments be intentional, not forceful.

Help him understand that just because I welcomed him, doesn't mean I'm not still adjusting too.

Shape him into a protector of my atmosphere,

A steward of my softness,

A man who doesn't just cohabitate — but cultivates.

In Jesus' name, Amen.

THIS AIN'T JUST HER HOUSE

Scripture Focus

> *"Be completely humble and gentle; be patient, bearing with one another in love. Make every effort to keep the unity of the Spirit through the bond of peace."*
>
> **Ephesians 4:2–3 (NIV)**

♫ Dedicated Song

"No Place Like You" — After 7

Love doesn't thrive in comfort — it grows in the spaces where two people choose unity over pride, surrender over control, and grace over preference.

Reflection

It's easy to prepare for a wedding. It's harder to prepare for the work of becoming one.

Moving in sounds like a simple step — but it's spiritual. Two lives. Two patterns. Two sets of rhythms, expectations, and habits suddenly converging under one roof. This isn't just about who folds the towels or which way the toilet paper hangs — it's about trust. About identity. About dying to self and building something together.

God isn't just watching how you lead when it's easy. He's watching how you adjust when it's hard. How you love in the ordinary. How you handle correction without defensiveness. How you respond when your comfort is challenged and your pride gets exposed.

The truth? You're not being diminished. You're being refined. **This isn't the death of your individuality — it's the birth of unity.**

Reflection Questions

1. What part of "moving in" challenged your sense of identity the most?

2. How did God use small moments to reveal deeper heart issues?

3. In what ways did humility or pride affect your ability to adjust?

4. What did you learn about healthy communication through shared space?

5. How can you reframe conflict as a tool for covenant instead of a threat to it?

Prayer

Lord, teach me how to love through humility.

Remind me that leadership includes listening.

Help me die to my pride and rise into Your purpose for this covenant.

Make our home a reflection of heaven — filled with grace, order, peace, and unity. In Jesus' name, Amen.

CHAPTER 10

THE BREAKING POINT

CHARLOTTESVILLE

"Let us not become weary in doing good, for at the proper time we will reap a harvest if we do not give up."
Galatians 6:9 (NIV)

This verse has always spoken to the heart of perseverance — to keep pressing forward, even when your soul is tired and your heart feels like it's breaking in silence. It's a promise that doing good is never wasted, that there's a harvest waiting for those who endure. But what do you do when the storm seems never-ending? When every attempt to hold things together feels like trying to grip water with your bare hands? When you're doing good, yet everything around you is still falling apart?

That was the Fourth of July weekend in 2024.

By then, the weight of coexisting under one roof had begun to take its toll. There were no explosive arguments, no scenes — but the air had grown heavy with tension. We were drifting, and

I could feel it. I thought maybe a change of scenery could help us find our way back. We had done it before — run to the mountains, to Charlottesville — a place that had always been a kind of sanctuary for us.

Charlottesville had been our reset button. A quiet escape filled with vineyards, peaceful roads, and the hush of the Blue Ridge Mountains watching over us. It was where we once held hands freely, laughed easily, and loved with intention. It wasn't just about getting away — it was about remembering who we were when the world wasn't so loud.

So, we packed our bags and left.

For a few moments, it worked. We laughed. We smiled. We sat across from each other at dinner and actually listened — really listened — to what the other was saying. For a brief window of time, it felt like we were reclaiming something we had lost. It felt like restoration was within reach.

But that feeling didn't last.

When we returned home, it was as if we had crossed back into a war zone — not one marked by yelling or chaos, but by distance and silence. Whatever peace we had found on that trip slipped through the cracks the moment we stepped over the threshold. I felt it leave her body like air escaping a balloon. And I felt something inside of me begin to collapse.

That's when the real storm hit — not loud, but loud enough to shake everything I thought was still standing.

You don't always see the breaking coming. Sometimes it's quiet. Sometimes it comes in the form of things unsaid, unmet expectations, or just the exhaustion of trying over and over with no sign that it's working. That weekend, I held onto hope like a man clinging to driftwood after a shipwreck. I believed the trip might have turned a corner for us. I believed we still had something to fight for.

But when we returned, I realized she had already begun to let go. And I was still fighting — alone.

That weekend now feels like a beautiful memory with a tragic aftertaste. A glimpse of what could've been ... followed by the reality of what was. It was the last time we laughed without trying. The last time we reached for each other without resistance. The last time I saw a future reflected in her eyes.

And still, Galatians 6:9 echoed in my soul: Don't grow weary. Don't give up. There is a harvest on the other side of this pain.

But when you're the only one planting seeds, and the soil feels dry, and the other gardener has walked away — what then?

Still, I press on. Not because I'm strong. But because God is.

Because even in the unraveling, I believe there's purpose.

Even when I feel forgotten, I believe He sees.

Even when love seems like it failed, I believe He still restores.

This is the tension of hope. This is what it means to believe when believing hurts. This is the kind of faith that bleeds.

And yet — I'm still here. Holding on. Planting. Waiting. Believing.

Back to routine, I returned to my job at the airport, exposed daily to crowds and travelers. Meanwhile, Hope started feeling sick — body aches, fever, deep fatigue.

COVID. Again.

This was her third time contracting it, and once again, the blame landed squarely on me. I had never tested positive. No symptoms. No illness. Yet, because of where I worked, Hope was convinced I was the carrier, bringing sickness into our home unknowingly.

Along with COVID, she struggled with recurring urinary tract infections, and somehow, that blame also found its way to me. But there was no medical evidence. No proof. Just the weight of suspicion.

Adding to it all, Hope was entering early menopause. Her body was changing in ways neither of us fully understood — emotional swings, physical discomfort, unpredictable health. I knew marriage demanded patience and compassion, especially in seasons of change. And I believed I was doing that. I believed I was being supportive, loving, attentive.

Even when she was sick, I tried to meet every need.

I ran errands.

I brought her food and medicine.

I made special trips to the store — like when her mother suggested coconut water. I thought I was being the husband she needed.

But something deeper was shifting.

Something I couldn't fix.

One morning, as she lay resting in bed, my heart ached watching her. So I did the only thing I knew to do: I prayed. I stood over her, lifting my hands in quiet prayer, asking God to heal her completely — from the top of her head to the soles of her feet. I poured out my heart in faith, believing that heaven would move.

As I prayed, she woke up.

She looked at me, confused. "What are you doing?" she asked.

"I'm praying for you," I said softly.

But instead of feeling comforted, her expression shifted — confusion, discomfort, maybe even fear. A wall seemed to rise between us.

Moments later, her mother arrived. She went upstairs to check on Hope. I didn't think much of it — until minutes later, they came downstairs carrying bags.

"Where are you going?" I asked, my stomach tightening.

"I just need to get my thoughts together," she said.

And just like that — she walked out the door.

She left — not just the house. She left *me*.

The home we built together. The space where prayers had been whispered. Where tears had been wiped away. Where laughter once lived. The place meant to be a new beginning ... now the setting of another heartbreak.

She walked away from the home she had lived in for 22 years. The place that was supposed to be a shared promise. A sacred ground for restoration.

And she didn't just leave the home — she left me.

I stood there, stunned. Not angry. Not yelling. Just ... hollow.

The silence in the air was suffocating — not because there was no noise, but because everything that should've been said ... wasn't.

The weight of her absence slammed into me like a familiar nightmare. Because I had been here before.

Years earlier, in my first marriage, I had watched my wife walk out with our children — watched the front door close behind the only people I called "home." That kind of pain doesn't fade. It hides. And when Hope left, it all came rushing back like a flood, swallowing me whole.

I stood in the middle of that house — our house — but suddenly, it felt like a stranger's walls. Every corner whispered memories I wasn't ready to relive. Every room echoed with silence that mocked me. The kitchen where we cooked. The couch where we prayed. The bed where we dreamed.

Gone.

I called. No answer.

I texted. Nothing.

I reached out with words soaked in desperation, but they vanished into the void like prayers hitting a locked heaven. The woman I had spoken to every day for four years — who once couldn't fall asleep without hearing my voice — now moved as if I had never existed.

Even her mother — who once called me "son" — now treated me like a stranger.

I wasn't just shut out. I was erased.

I stood there, broken … again.

The pain wasn't just in her leaving. It was in the suddenness of it all. The way I had gone from love to irrelevant. From husband to ghost. From chosen to forgotten.

And the question that clawed at my insides was simple — but impossible: Why?

Why did she leave without warning?

Why did love turn to silence?

Why did promises dissolve into avoidance?

And more personally — what was wrong with me that this was happening … again?

It wasn't just the absence of Hope from the house. It was the absence of hope in my soul.

Something inside me cracked in a way it hadn't before. Because this time, I had believed God was in it.

This time, I had prayed over every step. This time, I gave all I had. And still — I was left.

Left with memories that wouldn't let me sleep. Left with questions that wouldn't let me breathe. Left with a love that still beat loudly in a room now filled with silence.

I sat down on the edge of the bed we once shared, and for the first time in a long time, I realized: Some battles aren't fought with fists or words. They're fought in silence. In the tears you cry alone. In rooms that echo with what used to be. In the stillness that refuses to speak back.

And in that silence — I broke. Not because I was weak. But because I was human. Because I loved hard. Because I believed. And because when love leaves without a trace, the silence becomes its own kind of violence.

Yet even in that stillness ... I whispered one last prayer: "God, I don't understand. But I'm still Yours."

The hardest part wasn't the door closing. It wasn't the empty space where her bags used to be. It wasn't even the unanswered messages. The hardest part ... was knowing I couldn't fix it.

There were no magic words left. No acts of sacrifice to shift the outcome. No prayers loud enough to stop her from going.

This time, love didn't die in a fire. It slipped away quietly — like a slow leak in a tire, like a whisper you almost didn't hear, like breath fading in a dream.

I realized something that wrecked me: Brokenness doesn't always come with a warning. Sometimes it just ... leaves. It walks through the door with calm hands, packs its bags with no explanation, and vanishes while you're still believing things might turn around.

And there I was — left standing in a house that still held her scent ... but not her presence.

A home that once felt like restoration, now echoing with silence so loud it pierced my soul.

And in that silence — in the stillness where I couldn't hear her voice anymore — I heard another voice. Gentle. Firm. Unmistakable.

Will you still trust Me?

I froze, because I knew this wasn't just a question — it was a crossroads.

Trust meant surrendering the need for closure. Trust meant releasing my grip on how the story "should" end. Trust meant believing God was still good, even if the ending wasn't the one I prayed for.

Every part of me wanted to demand answers. But somewhere deeper — past the ache, past the fear — I knew this was the only question that mattered.

Not because the outcome made sense. Not because I had understanding. Not because restoration seemed likely. But because faith isn't measured in the comfort of answered prayers — it's proven in the aching spaces between them.

Faith is forged when you're standing in the wreckage, holding nothing but your shattered heart, and choosing to believe that even this — even this unbearable, suffocating pain — isn't the end of your story.

Brother to Brother:
When the Storm Breaks You, Don't Let It Bury You

To the man sitting in silence, staring at the door she walked out of — I see you.

You gave your best. You prayed over her. You served her. You stayed faithful through frustration, sickness, shifting moods, and changing seasons. And still — she left.

Now you're standing in the ruins of what was supposed to be sacred. And it hurts like hell.

Brother, hear me: This pain doesn't mean you failed. It means you were *all in*. And being all in will sometimes break you in ways you didn't see coming.

The worst kind of hurt isn't betrayal by an enemy — it's abandonment by someone who once called you *home.*

It's the silence after four years of consistent love. It's praying for her healing and watching her pack a bag instead. It's realizing that no matter how much you give, you can't make someone stay.

But here's the truth you need to grab hold of right now: Your value is not measured by who walks away. Your faith is not void just because it wasn't enough to fix it. And your purpose didn't die in that empty room.

God is still present — even when your house is empty. He's still speaking — even when your phone is silent. And He's still working — even when your heart is barely holding together.

Brother, you're not crazy for loving deeply. You're not weak for crying. You're not broken beyond repair because you got left again. You're human. You're healing. You're His.

So, what do you do now?

- You feel the pain — don't fake it.

- You pray anyway — even when it feels like God is quiet.

- You trust without understanding — because *that's* what faith actually is.

- And you keep breathing — even if it's just one hour at a time. Because the same God who saw you at the altar sees you now in the aftermath. And He still has a plan.

This isn't the end of your story. It's the breaking point — but not the breaking of you. It's the place where God strips everything — so He can rebuild you stronger.

So, don't numb it. Don't rush it. Don't run from it. Stand in it.

And when all you can do is whisper one last prayer through your tears, let it be this: "God, I don't understand. But I still trust You." Because that, my brother, is the kind of faith that moves mountains — even when all you can see are ashes.

Brother to Sister:
Pray When He's Been Left Without Closure

Sis, it's hard to watch a strong man break. Not because of failure — but because of faithfulness. Because he showed up. Because he prayed. Because he believed in restoration. And she still walked away.

That kind of heartbreak doesn't make headlines. It often happens in silence, behind closed doors, while the world assumes he's fine.

But you know better. You know that behind his quiet strength might be a soul screaming for answers. You know that behind the calm might be questions he doesn't have words for. You know that love didn't fail him — but it did leave him.

So, don't just pray for his healing — Pray for his identity to survive this storm.

Pray this over him:

Lord, I lift up the man who gave his all and was still left behind.

I pray not just for comfort — but for restoration in his soul.

Remind him that this heartbreak isn't the end of his story.

That he's not broken beyond repair.

That his value isn't defined by the one who walked away.

When he questions everything, be his steady.

When he wants to shut down, be his breath.

Strip the lies.

Silence the shame.

*And anchor him in the truth that he is still Yours —
still chosen, still seen, still called.*

I pray he finds peace in the pieces.

*I pray he learns to rest, even when nothing makes
sense.*

*I pray that in the emptiness, he finds You all over
again.*

In Jesus' name, Amen.

WHEN THE GLOW FADES

Scripture Focus

"Watch and pray so that you will not fall into temptation. The spirit is willing, but the flesh is weak."

Matthew 26:41 (NIV)

♫ Dedicated Song

"Rainman" — Jamie Foxx

What do you do when the truth ain't enough? You hold on when nobody's holdin' you up.

Reflection

What do you do when love doesn't feel as easy as it once did?

There's a moment in every marriage when the glow starts to dim — not because the love is gone, but because real life has set in. And the enemy doesn't usually attack through a full-on storm. He sneaks in through silence. Through subtle disconnection. Through unspoken frustration.

The danger isn't always betrayal. Sometimes it's neglect. Sometimes it's pride. Sometimes it's distraction. And sometimes … it's simply not praying together like you used to.

This season of love requires watching and praying — guarding your heart, not just from outside temptation, but from internal drifting. The glow fading isn't always a sign of failure. It's an invitation to fight — not with fists, but with faith:

- To love when it's not convenient.

- To pursue when it's not reciprocated.

- To serve when it feels one-sided.

- And to pray, even when it feels like you're praying alone.

Reflection Questions

1. What small signs revealed the emotional or spiritual drift in your relationship?

2. How did silence — yours or hers — begin to shift the dynamic of your connection?

3. What role did prayer (or lack of it) play in your ability to navigate this season?

4. In what ways did you try to fix the surface without addressing the root?

5. What does "watching and praying" look like for you right now?

Prayer

Lord, help me not to become numb to what You joined together.

Open my eyes to subtle drift.

Sharpen my sensitivity to love not with emotion alone, but with endurance.

Bring light where things have dimmed. Restore what we've lost.

Remind me that real love doesn't quit — it watches and prays. In Jesus' name, Amen.

CHAPTER 11

FAITH IN THE SILENCE

"The Lord is good to those whose hope is in him, to the one who seeks him; it is good to wait quietly for the salvation of the Lord."

Lamentations 3:25–26 (NIV)

When God is quiet, He is not absent. He is working in shadows too sacred for us to see.

There's a kind of silence that doesn't just surround you — it stretches inside of you. It doesn't rush in like a storm. It creeps in slowly, subtly, like fog weaving between your thoughts. After Hope left, it wasn't just the absence of her voice or her footsteps. It was the vacancy her absence created — not just in the house, but in my soul. I wasn't prepared for how loud quiet could be. It wasn't just the lack of conversation or routine. It was the disappearance of certainty. Her leaving dismantled my rhythm, disoriented my prayers, and left me pacing rooms where love once lived, unsure of what I even believed anymore.

I used to talk about trusting God like it was muscle memory. Faith had always been my default setting. I knew all the scriptures. I had declared them over others, stood on them myself. But now they sat in my spirit like echoes from a distant room— faint, familiar, but no longer loud.

When the storm came, I expected rescue. Instead, I got silence. Not the kind that comforts. The kind that confronts. I realized how much I had equated God's voice with His approval. I thought peace meant progress. I assumed clarity meant closeness. I realized I had confused the presence of peace with the presence of progress, assuming God's voice always meant His approval. But the wilderness stripped away those comforts and exposed the unspoken truth: I could no longer feel the God I had always loved.

Spiritual warfare in this season didn't look like demons in the dark. It looked like depression in the daylight. It wasn't nightmares. It was numbness. Waking up and not recognizing your own life — or worse, not wanting to keep living it. The battlefield wasn't around me. It was inside me. And every morning, I entered an internal courtroom where the accusations never stopped: You failed. You lost her. You're not who you thought you were. God went silent because you blew it.

These weren't battles fought on my knees — they were fought in my mind. When no one else was around. When the only voice I could hear was the one trying to convince me I was disqualified, discarded, forgotten. And yet ... I couldn't let go. Maybe it was stubborn faith. Maybe it was spiritual reflex. Or maybe it was the Spirit of God, flickering like a pilot light that simply refused to go out.

It's a strange thing to walk with God and yet not feel Him. To serve a speaking God who suddenly feels mute. But I began to realize something deeper: God's silence didn't mean He was gone. When He hides, it's often because He's building. There's a trial few talk about — the trial of divine restraint. When God doesn't pull you out. When He lets the furnace keep burning. When He allows the silence to stretch until it scrapes against your sanity. Not to punish — but to prepare. To hollow out the noise so that when His voice finally breaks through, it lands with holy weight. This wasn't punishment. This was precision. This was pruning.

The silence taught me to stop performing. To stop trying to earn my healing. It taught me that brokenness is not something to hide from God — but something to hand Him. It reminded me that I am not loved because I'm functional. I'm loved because I'm His. And in that quiet place, stripped of roles and results, I had to face the hardest question: If God never restores what I lost, would I still call Him good? That's where a different kind of faith was born. Not the faith that shouts from pulpits — but the kind that whispers from caves. The kind that says, *Even if You don't come through for me, I'll stay right here.* Because real faith doesn't always roar. Sometimes it simply survives the silence.

God's silence wasn't the end of a chapter. It was the pause before something sacred. The lull before resurrection. When something holy is forming, heaven often turns down the volume. The enemy tried to convince me that the silence meant God was gone. But in truth, it meant God was near — closer than I could comprehend. Being formed hurts. It's not poetic when you're in it. But formation always requires stillness. And when God finally spoke — it wasn't thunder. It was a whisper. A whisper that pierced the ruins of my identity and said, "You are still Mine."

Hope had begun coming back to the house — but only when I wasn't home. Slipping in during the day to gather her things. I knew it was happening. I said nothing. I thought maybe space could bring clarity. Maybe silence could still become healing. I still believed in restoration. Still believed this was temporary. But then I came home and noticed the Wi-Fi was disconnected. Just a minor detail. But symbolic. It was no longer a drift. It was a severing. She wasn't just leaving. She was deleting me. I wrote her an email. Not to fight. Just to express. To plead. I asked her — stop playing with my heart. Stop dismantling our covenant while pretending there's still hope. I wasn't looking for drama. I was reaching for peace.

What came next shattered me. She took my words — words born from grief — and reported them as a threat. She told the authorities I was unstable. Dangerous. Then came the knock.

Police. Paperwork. A protective order. I was no longer a husband. I was now a threat on paper. A liability. A file in a system.

In court, she looked at the judge and said, "He was praying over me. I felt a tingling. I think ... he poisoned me."

Poisoned? She told her mother, "If anything happens to me, get a toxicology report."

I couldn't believe what I was hearing. Intercession — prayer — now seen as evidence of harm. The sacred became suspicious. My tears weren't seen as grief. They were dismissed as performance.

"Elton can cry on demand," she said. "He knows how to put on a show."

That didn't just hurt. It hollowed me. It stripped me of my right to feel.

The judge granted the order. And I walked out of that courtroom no longer a man fighting for marriage. I was a man accused. A man erased. The betrayal wasn't just personal. It was spiritual. My love was rewritten as control. My covenant was repackaged as a threat. My prayers were now poison. And the wound it carved in me? Only God could reach it.

When I got home, I found out why she was late to court. She had sent movers. Our life — our memories — scattered across the lawn like discarded debris. Shoes. Books. Pictures. Clothes. All of it. Even my dog — chained in the backyard, barking in confusion. I tried to open the front door. But the key didn't work.

The locks had been changed. The door was shut. So was her heart. And I collapsed.

I stared at my wedding ring. What once symbolized forever now felt like a cruel joke. I wanted to throw it. Scream. Do something. Anything. But a friend caught me in that moment. "Don't make a permanent choice from a temporary storm," he said. I dropped the ring into his hand. Not because I believed him. But because I didn't trust myself.

That night, I sat in my car. No music. No movement. Just silence. But inside, everything was unraveling. I realized I had confused the presence of peace with the presence of progress, assuming God's voice always meant His approval. Then a voice came — so quiet, so reasonable, it almost made sense: *Just end it. You're already gone in her eyes. Finish the story.*

It wasn't demonic. It was logical. It sounded like relief. And I almost listened.

I gripped the steering wheel, my breath uneven, my mind dangling on the edge of surrender. One more second and I might have done it. Hurt comes in many ways and what I was experiencing I wish that on no one.

But then another Voice. Firm. Gentle. Familiar. *No. Not yet. This is not the end.* It wasn't me. It wasn't my friend. It was God. And in that moment, I broke. I didn't just cry. I wept from my soul. Because I realized what the silence had tried to make me forget: God never left. Even when the world turned against me.

Even when lies drowned out truth. Even when my name was slandered and my hands were empty.

He stayed.

His voice didn't shame me. It rescued me. And in that darkest night of my life, a seed of light was planted. Tiny. Fragile. Almost invisible. But alive.

And sometimes … all it takes is one whisper from heaven to keep you breathing.

Brother to Brother: Fighting on Your Knees

To the man reading this with tears on your pillow and war in your mind — This is for you.

To the one bleeding silently through the cracks of your smile — This is your battle cry.

I know what it's like to have your whole world collapse without warning. To stand in the rubble of everything you thought was sacred and ask, "How did we get here?"

One day you're building dreams. The next, you're sifting through ashes.

And the silence in your home? It's not just quiet — it's suffocating.

But hear me, Brother: this is not the end of your story. The enemy wants you to believe that because your wife left, because people walked away, because your name was dragged and your heart was shattered — God must be done with you.

That is a lie.

That voice? That's not the voice of your Father. That's the accuser. That's the thief. That's the voice that wants to bury you before your resurrection.

But I'm telling you — he wouldn't be fighting you this hard if you weren't still dangerous. You are a threat to darkness.

This isn't punishment. It's preparation.

This isn't a grave. It's a garden.

God is not trying to kill you — He's trying to rebuild you. He is pruning what can't go with you. Breaking you free from false dependencies. Pulling you back to your true foundation — Him.

You are not too broken. You are not too late. You are not disqualified.

You are still chosen. Still anointed. Still a son.

But now — it's time to fight differently. Not with fists — with faith. Not with anger — with surrender.

Fall to your knees. Cry if you must. Groan if words won't come. Because God hears the cries of His sons.

> *"The righteous cry out, and the Lord hears them; He delivers them from all their troubles."*
>
> **Psalm 34:17 (NIV)**

He hears you. Even when the prayer is a whisper. Even when the only words you can form are, *God ... please.*

And He is moving. Right now. Making a way in the wilderness. Carving rivers in your desert. Rebuilding ruins with resurrection power.

So, rise — not in your strength, but in His. Put on your armor, even if your hands shake. Pick up your sword, even if your grip is weak.

Stand your ground, even if your knees buckle — because heaven stands with you.

This is not your burial. It's your rebirth.

Your scars will become your sermon. Your wounds will carry wisdom.

And this battle? It will be the birthplace of your boldness.

Don't bow out. Don't give up. Don't believe the lie that it's over.

Because this is where the comeback begins. Where your story becomes a weapon. Where your knees become your altar. And where your cry becomes your catalyst for victory.

Brother to Sister:
Pray When He's Surrounded by Silence
and Misunderstanding

Sis, there will be moments in his life when he is buried beneath silence — not just the kind without words, but the kind where it feels like even God isn't speaking. Where people don't believe him. Where loved ones misread him. Where his reputation is attacked and his heart is on trial.

In those moments, the man of God you've been praying for may not need answers — he'll need *covering*. He'll need someone who can see past the accusations and pray him through the isolation.

This is not a time to fix him. This is a time to fight for him in the Spirit.

Pray this over him:

Lord, I lift up the man who is being falsely seen but truly broken.

Not many know the weight he's carrying.

Not many understand the silence he's walking through.

So I stand in the gap for him.

I cover his name. I cover his heart. I cover his mind.

I pray that the lies spoken against him would not take root in his spirit.

I pray that shame will not have the final word.

I pray that confusion will not take his voice.

When he feels abandoned — remind him You are near.

When he's tempted to doubt himself — remind him of who he is in You.

Let this silence be a sanctuary, not a sentence.

Let this darkness be a doorway, not a dead end.

And when he has no one to speak for him, let Heaven be his defense.

In Jesus' name, Amen.

WHEN GOD IS SILENT

Scripture Focus

"Be still before the Lord and wait patiently for Him ..."
Psalm 37:7 (NIV)

♪ Dedicated Song

"Even When It Hurts" (Praise Song) Live — Hillsong UNITED

Sometimes the purest praise rises not from victory — but from agony. This song is a reminder that even in the silence, even in the sorrow, worship is still a weapon.

Reflection

It's one thing to walk through a storm. It's another to walk through it in silence.

There are seasons when heaven feels like it's on mute. You pray — and hear nothing. You seek clarity — but get confusion. You ask for direction — and only receive delay.

And in those moments, the enemy will whisper: God has forgotten you. He brought you this far just to leave you here.

But that's a lie.

God's silence is not His absence. His delays are not His denials. And His stillness doesn't mean He's stopped moving.

Sometimes, God doesn't speak because He's building. Sometimes, the silence is where you unlearn the need for control and learn the rhythm of trust.

Sometimes, it's in the silence that faith becomes more than a word — it becomes your lifeline.

Reflection Questions

1. What emotions did you wrestle with most when your prayers felt unanswered?

2. How did the silence affect your sense of identity and your view of God?

3. Were there moments where you began to doubt the entire journey? Why?

4. How is God maturing your faith through silence — not just testing it?

5. What does it look like for you to wait with *hope*, not just endurance?

Prayer

Father, even when You are silent — I will wait.

Even when I don't feel You — I will trust.

Help me rest in the truth that You are still working behind the scenes.

Give me the strength to be faithful in the silence, and peace that surpasses understanding. In Jesus' name, Amen.

CHAPTER 12

RESTORATION'S TRUE FACE

"All this is from God, who reconciled us to himself through Christ and gave us the ministry of reconciliation."

2 Corinthians 5:18 (NIV)

We often think restoration means getting back what was lost — retracing steps to recover something familiar, something we held dear. We imagine it like a movie ending, a beautiful rewind. But God doesn't do rewinds. He does resurrections. He doesn't return us to what was. He redeems what is and resurrects what could be.

Restoration isn't about picking up the pieces and putting them back the same way. It's about becoming something new, something stronger, something holy.

What we usually pray for is reversal. We want the relationship restored, the job back, the peace we once knew. But God isn't in the business of replicating our past. He uses the fire, the wreckage, the silence — all of it — as raw material. He builds something greater, not by avoiding the pain, but by entering it. Not to patch it up, but to rebuild the foundation underneath it.

Healing isn't God restoring the appearance of what was. It's Him planting something deeper beneath the rubble. It's Him building an identity that isn't shaken by people leaving or promises breaking. It's Him saying, "I'm not trying to return you to who you were. I'm introducing you to who you are." And that truth unraveled me. Because I didn't want to become anything new — I just wanted my life back. I wanted her back. I wanted peace. But instead of giving me what I wanted, God gave me what I needed — Himself.

The restoration I thought I needed was external. But what God was after was internal. He wasn't just interested in reconciling me with Hope. He was reconciling me to Himself. He was rebuilding my faith. Restoring my voice. Refusing to let my identity be determined by a title, a ring, or a courtroom. He didn't wait for me to get over it. He met me in the middle of it — and whispered, *You are still mine.*

And that began to change everything. Because real restoration doesn't always look like reunion. Sometimes it looks like standing in the ruins with peace that makes no sense. Sometimes it looks like smiling through tears. Sometimes it looks like praying for the one who hurt you. And sometimes … it just looks like breathing when you don't want to.

I'm now standing thirty days from what might be the final hearing. It doesn't feel like paperwork. It feels like a funeral. Like I'm watching a covenant laid in the ground with no promise of resurrection. I did everything I could. I prayed when the words ran out. I fasted when food couldn't comfort me. I worshipped through sobbing. I stood when I could barely stay upright. I loved when it wasn't returned. And still ... it might end here.

But somewhere in that heartbreak, God asked me the question that changed everything: What if restoration doesn't mean your marriage gets saved? What if restoration is happening — even now — even if she never comes back? That question crushed me. It felt like betrayal at first. But then I realized — it wasn't a betrayal. It was a breaking open. Because I had attached God's goodness to one single outcome. And when that outcome seemed to die, I questioned everything. But God isn't a transaction. He's a Father. He's not trying to make deals with my devotion — He's after my heart.

And sometimes, in His mercy, He withholds what we want to give us what we were made for. Sometimes He delays reconciliation because He's developing revelation. Sometimes what we think is a dead end is actually the doorway to becoming. I still love her because He calls me to love her the way He does. I still hope. But I also see now — God didn't just want to fix my marriage. He wanted to free me. From needing a result to believe in

His presence. From tying my worth to what stays or what leaves. From performing instead of trusting.

The story of Joseph is never far from me. I remember one night, at my lowest point, sitting with my Bible open but barely able to read through the tears. My eyes fell on Joseph's story — not because I was looking for it, but because God put it in front of me. And for the first time, I didn't read it like a Sunday school lesson. I read it like a mirror. He was betrayed by his own blood. Sold like property. Lied on. Imprisoned. Forgotten. Years passed. Dreams felt dead.

Yet God was not sleeping. Heaven was staging. Every injustice became a stepping stone. Every silence, a setup. Joseph wasn't returned to his old life. He was elevated to one that didn't even seem possible. And when given the chance to get even, he didn't seek vengeance. He chose grace. Not because they deserved it — because he had become someone different.

And I see now — maybe my marriage wasn't the destination. Maybe it was the soil. Maybe the betrayal didn't break my calling. Maybe it birthed it. And if Joseph's pit didn't cancel God's promise, then neither does mine. My heart still aches. But now I ask God not just to restore what I lost, but to reveal why I'm still here. I want to steward the pit like it matters. I want to carry the palace with clean hands. And if all of this was preparation for what's ahead, then let it be holy. Let the pain become purpose.

There was a time when I believed that loving someone meant fixing everything. If something was broken, I'd shoulder the repair. But somewhere along the way, God showed me — I'm not the owner. I'm the steward. I don't control the outcome. I carry the assignment. And sometimes that means praying without results. Loving without response. Honoring when it costs everything. Because love is not ownership. It's trust. It's saying, *God, I did all I could. Now I leave the rest in Your hands.*

She was never mine. She is God's daughter. Before she was my wife, she was His child. And that truth reshapes how I speak about her. How I pray for her. How I think about what was and what might never be again. Even now, in silence and separation, I am still called to honor her. Not because she earned it — but because God commanded it. Because covenant love doesn't die with disappointment. It lives in obedience.

And this kind of love — agape love — costs more than I expected. It crucifies pride. It lays down rights. It whispers in the dark, *Love anyway.* It prays when there's no reply. It refuses to curse what it once called holy. It's not built on chemistry. It's rooted in covenant. It's not powered by reciprocation. It's sustained by God. And it hurts. Oh, it hurts. But it also heals.

Because when you love like Jesus, you're not driven by results. You're anchored by the cross. And this love … it cannot be faked. It's forged in silence. It's baptized in tears. And I've found it — not in a romantic moment, but in a spiritual surrender. In the quiet. In the absence. In the ache. I've found the grace to love her — not because she's loving me — but because God is loving through me.

And now, as the final court date draws near, the weight I carry is more than paperwork. It's the pressure of releasing a dream I never wanted to die. But I've learned — surrender feels like death before it feels like freedom. And sometimes, the bravest thing you can do is let go of what you can't control and hold onto the One who never changes. So I say, God, even if it ends here, let it begin with You. Even if the promise looks buried, let my worship rise. Even if I never see restoration the way I prayed for it, let me become the man You saw when You allowed it all to break.

This isn't the story of failure. It's the story of formation. God hasn't wasted a single tear. Not the love. Not the longing. Not the silence. He's been writing something deeper than I ever planned. And now, I no longer trust the outcome — I trust the Author.

> **"For I know the plans I have for you," declares the Lord, "plans to prosper you and not to harm you, plans to give you a hope and a future."**
> **Jeremiah 29:11 (NIV)**

Since she left, something strange has happened — I've grown. She helped plant seeds she may never see bloom. She challenged my health, my habits, my spiritual discipline. She saw something in me I couldn't see in myself. And now, I'm living in the fruit of that challenge. But here's the hard part — she might never witness it.

I thought growth needed her applause. But I was wrong. True growth is measured not by who claps — but by who sustains it. I'm not living for her affirmation anymore. I'm living for His. Because even if she doesn't see the man I've become, God sees. And that's enough.

She helped water it. But God is growing it. And maybe ... just maybe ... that was the point all along. Because even without the ending I imagined, I've found something I never expected — peace. And in His hands, even my deepest fall has become a safe place to land.

THE GOD WHO STAYS

Scripture Focus

"The Lord is close to the brokenhearted and saves those who are crushed in spirit."

Psalm 34:18 (NIV)

♫ Dedicated Song

"Make Room" (Lyrics) — Community Music

True restoration begins at the altar of surrender. This song isn't just background — it's the sound of letting go, the sound of God doing holy work in hidden places.

Reflection

There are moments when life hits so hard, you can't breathe — when everything you prayed for, everything you worked for, crumbles in your hands.

You did it God's way.

You believed.

You fought for the covenant.

And still … it fell apart.

It's in these moments when the enemy whispers: *You're alone. God walked away too. You must have failed.*

But the truth? God is closer than He's ever been. He doesn't walk away when others do. He doesn't leave when the house goes silent. He kneels in the dust with you — right where your tears fall.

This kind of heartbreak strips everything away until all that's left is raw faith. But raw faith is real faith. And real faith is the soil where healing begins.

Even when the covenant broke ... God didn't. Even when she left ... He stayed. And what you build from here won't come from striving — it will come from surrender.

Reflection Questions

1. What did the end of your marriage reveal about your view of God's love for you?

2. Were there lies you began to believe about yourself in the middle of that loss?

3. How did God meet you — not in the fix, but in the fracture?

4. What does surrender look like when restoration doesn't come the way you imagined?

5. How is your faith changing — not by being strong, but by being *honest*?

Prayer

Lord, I don't understand this loss. I don't see the reason. But I trust that You are still good.

You are the God who stays. The God who heals. The God who restores.

I give You my pain. My disappointment. My broken dreams.

Breathe new life into the ashes.

Make beauty out of this breaking.

And lead me into healing. In Jesus' name, Amen.

WHEN GOD WRITES THE STORY

God's plan may break your heart before it blesses you. It may strip away everything familiar before it reveals what's eternal. It may feel like silence, like abandonment, like loss — But what feels like the end is often just the beginning of becoming.

His path may confuse you before it clarifies you. His delays may feel like denials. His pruning may feel like punishment. But in the confusion, He is clearing the noise. In the silence, He is refining your ears to hear. In the breaking, He is making room for glory.

He is not absent. He is not indifferent. He is not finished.

He is refining you. He is aligning you. He is preparing you. Not just for restoration of what was — but for the unveiling of who you were always meant to be.

So, when the dust settles … When the papers are signed … When the door you prayed would open remains closed and you find yourself standing on the other side of the storm with nothing but your faith — You will see it.

You'll look back and realize:

- His plan was higher than yours.

- His love reached deeper than your pain.

- His restoration wasn't about rebuilding what broke — it was about resurrecting you.

Even if your marriage ends in court, your story does not end in defeat. Because God doesn't end in ashes. He begins there.

He is still restoring. He is still redeeming. He is still God.

So, stand firm, Brother. Even if you stand alone. Even if your prayers go unanswered in the way you hoped. Even if the world misunderstands your faith and your silence is mocked.

Stand.

Because the cross looked like the end, too. It looked like failure. It looked like silence had won. It looked like death had the final word.

But it wasn't the end. It was the greatest beginning in human history. And just like the tomb was empty three days later, so too will your pain give way to purpose. So, too, will your ashes give rise to beauty.

So, too, will your story reflect the Author who never wastes a single page.

You were never alone in this. And this — this — was never the end.

THE HEALING BEGINS

As I write this, I find myself less than thirty days from what could be the final hearing. And with every passing day, I sit with a grief deeper than I expected. It isn't just the legal finality of divorce — it is the weight of what could have been, the ache of what was lost, and the silent mourning of a covenant that once felt unbreakable.

This journey has been the most vulnerable chapter of my life. Before marriage, I had never opened up in this way. I had never let my guard down long enough for someone to truly see my wounds. But marriage forced me to confront myself. And divorce ... divorce forced me to confront God.

I've learned that vulnerability is not weakness — it's the beginning of true healing. Through these pages, I haven't offered a polished version of my life. I've chosen to give you the raw truth — the mess, the moments of despair, and the miracle of still standing. Because men do hurt. And yes, men do cry. But most of us were never taught how to mourn out loud. We were told to hold it in, to push it down, to keep moving.

But emotions buried alive don't die. They resurface in other ways — violence, silence, withdrawal, rage. I've had to face that in myself. I've thrown things. I've said words I wish I could take back. But those reactions weren't strength. They were symptoms of suppressed pain. And that's not who God created me to be. That's not the reflection of Christ I want to carry.

In January 2025, the final court date came and went. I prayed. I wept. I fasted. I pleaded for restoration.

Then God asked me a question I never saw coming: What if restoration doesn't mean the marriage is saved? What if restoration is happening — even if she never returns?

That question shifted everything. It peeled back the layers of my theology, my expectations, and my pain. Because somewhere along the way, I had begun to equate restoration with a specific outcome. I thought if I prayed hard enough, surrendered long enough, and stayed faithful, the story had to end in reconciliation. But God doesn't promise us formulas — He invites us into faith.

Now I see that restoration isn't always about getting back what was lost. Sometimes, it's about discovering what was buried. It's about becoming someone who can carry peace even when the storm doesn't subside. It's about healing in the silence, finding purpose in the pain, and learning to love again — starting with yourself.

Yes, I still believe in miracles. I still believe God can do the impossible. But I've also come to believe that I am the miracle — that the man who emerged from this fire is not the same man who entered it. He is softer, wiser, more surrendered. And that is restoration in its truest form.

So, if God sees fit to reunite what was broken — I'll be ready. But if He doesn't — I will still worship.

Because now I understand: the real restoration was never just about a relationship.

It was about me being restored to God.

And that alone is worth it all.

I've spent nearly a year writing this book. And in many ways, I haven't been able to start healing until now. The process has been raw. It has forced me to relive trauma, to wrestle with truth, and to face myself on the page. But I needed that. Because healing doesn't begin when the pain ends — it begins when we stop pretending we're not hurting.

This book is not just a testimony. It's a turning point.

And if God so chooses to restore my marriage one day, I'll walk into that future with open hands, not clenched fists — because restoration won't be a rewind. It'll be a resurrection.

If you've made it to this point, thank you for walking this journey with me.

My prayer is that these pages become a safe place for you, too.

A place to grieve.

A place to believe.

A place to heal.

— E. J. Hutchison, *A Safe Place to Land*

ACKNOWLEDGMENTS

I would like to take a moment to acknowledge the people who have stood with me, supported me, and poured into my life throughout this journey. None of what I have accomplished would be possible without the love, guidance, and encouragement I've received from those who mean the most to me.

To my parents, Elton Hutchison Sr. and Gwendolyn Hutchison — there are no words great enough to capture the depth of my gratitude and love for you both. From the very beginning, you laid the foundation upon which my life continues to stand — a foundation built on faith, discipline, love, and integrity. You have been my constant examples of what true strength, perseverance, and grace look like, even in the face of life's greatest challenges.

You taught me that character matters more than circumstance, that faith can move mountains, and that love — when it's rooted in God — can carry you through anything. You showed me how to work hard, to walk with humility, and to treat others with kindness and respect. Those lessons have guided me through every chapter of my life and have become the compass that leads me still.

Your sacrifices have not gone unnoticed. Every opportunity I've been blessed to experience, every success I've achieved, stands as a reflection of your unwavering dedication and the countless prayers you have spoken over my life. You gave of yourselves selflessly so that I could grow, dream, and believe in what's possible.

Mom, your gentle spirit, endless patience, and nurturing heart have been my safe place. Dad, your strength, your wisdom, and your steadfast faith have been my anchor. Together, you have shown me what it truly means to build a life grounded in love, respect, and devotion — to one another, to family, and to God.

Everything I am today, and everything I strive to become, is because of the foundation you built and the example you set. I am forever grateful for the honor of being your child. Thank you for loving me, believing in me, and showing me the power of faith, family, and unconditional love.

To my brother, Anthony J. Hutchison — I dedicate this book to you. As my older brother, you always bestowed upon me wisdom, love, and unwavering support in everything I pursued. Though it saddens me that you're not here to witness the fruition of this project, I am certain that your spirit rejoices in its purpose—reaching and healing others, and setting them free.

You have always had a heart for people, and I believe that compassion and empathy are qualities I've inherited from you. These values resonate through every page and every chapter of this book.

You will forever be missed and loved, and I look forward to the day we reunite. Until then, your spirit and the impact you've had on my life will always remain.

I love you.

To my daughter, Azanaa Hutchison — you are my heartbeat, my greatest inspiration, and my most beautiful blessing. Your life fuels my purpose and gives meaning to every step I take. Watching you grow, learn, and blossom into the remarkable young woman you are becoming fills my heart with indescribable pride and joy. Every milestone you reach, every dream you chase, reminds me that love, faith, and perseverance truly shape destiny.

You are the reason I strive to be better every single day — to push beyond limits, to dream beyond boundaries, and to live with purpose and integrity. Your light shines so brightly, even in moments when you don't realize it. You embody strength, grace, and resilience, and through you, I am constantly reminded of what's possible when we lead with love and courage.

Never forget, Azanaa, that you carry greatness within you. You were created to stand tall, to lead, to love deeply, and to make an impact in this world. I am endlessly proud of the woman you are becoming — not just for what you achieve, but for the beautiful spirit, compassion, and wisdom that already radiate from you.

You are my daughter, my joy, and my forever inspiration. I thank God every day for the gift of you.

To Shana Gasper — you are one of the strongest and most resilient people I know. Your life is a true testament to courage, perseverance, and grace under pressure. Despite the daily challenges you face with your health, and the demands of raising your son while balancing work, you continue to stand tall with unwavering faith and determination.

Even in the midst of your own battles, you have found the strength to pour into me — offering love, encouragement, and wisdom during some of my darkest days. Your compassion runs deep, and your ability to lift others even when you are carrying your own weight is nothing short of extraordinary.

I am profoundly grateful for your presence in my life — for your honesty, your heart, and your unwavering support. You remind me that true strength isn't just about surviving hardships, but about doing so with kindness, humility, and love. Thank you for being who you are, and for continuing to shine your light so boldly.

To Onyx — my loyal companion, my steadfast protector, and my constant source of comfort. For the past eight years, you have walked beside me through every season of my life. You've been there through moments of joy and triumph, and you've stood faithfully through the storms — never wavering, never judging, always present. You have witnessed the best and the hardest parts of my journey, and in it all, you have loved me unconditionally.

Your loyalty is beyond words. You have been my strength when I was weak, my calm when the world felt heavy, and my joy when I needed a reason to smile. You have an extraordinary gift — to sense what I need before I even speak it. Your quiet presence has brought me peace on the toughest days, and your playful spirit has reminded me that even in the midst of struggle, there is still light, laughter, and love.

You are more than a service dog — you are family, a true blessing sent to walk this path with me. The bond we share transcends words; it is one of trust, devotion, and unspoken understanding. You have taught me patience, reminded me to breathe, and shown me that love knows no language — it is simply felt.

Onyx, thank you for every step you've taken beside me, for every moment you've guarded my heart, and for the countless ways you've made life brighter just by being in it. You will always hold a special place in my heart, my forever friend and faithful partner. **Ruff-ruff!** 🐾

To Ayanna Brown — in your youthfulness lies a wisdom and grace that far exceed your years. You carry yourself with the strength, dignity, and poise of a seasoned wife and mother — a woman grounded in faith and guided by divine purpose. Your life is a reflection of what it means to walk as a true woman of

God — steady in conviction, pure in heart, and unwavering in your devotion to family and faith.

Your insight into the sacred responsibility of what family is meant to be — rooted in love, anchored in faith, and built upon the Word — is both rare and remarkable. You understand that the foundation of a Godly home begins not just in structure, but in spirit. You live that truth daily, setting an example not only for your own household, but for every woman who watches and learns from your quiet strength and radiant grace.

You inspire me, Ayanna. Your life reminds me that a Godly woman's power does not come from outward appearances or worldly success, but from her heart — a heart surrendered to God, a mind renewed by His Word, and a spirit that walks in obedience and humility.

It is a blessing to share the same Christian understanding with you — to stand in agreement on what it means to honor God through our lives, our families, and our womanhood. You are a light to your generation — a living testimony that faith, love, and purpose can coexist beautifully when God is at the center.

Thank you for being an example of grace, strength, and spiritual excellence. You are not only admired but deeply respected, and I am grateful for the inspiration you bring into my life.

To Adonica Franklin — our friendship spans decades, beginning in elementary school, and through all those years, you have seen me grow from a curious child into the man I am today.

Through every stage of life, you have been a constant presence —
a sister in spirit, a confidante, and a guiding force.

There were times when we disagreed, times when we clashed,
and times when we stood completely in sync — yet through it all,
one thing has never wavered: your heart toward me. Your love,
care, and unwavering desire for my best have been evident, even
when I could not see it for myself. You have consistently shown
me what it means to be selfless, loyal, and invested in someone
else's life in the truest sense of friendship.

I also want to express my gratitude to your husband, Ter-
rance, and your son, Harlem, for sharing you with me. Your love
and support for your family have never diminished your gen-
erosity of spirit, and I am profoundly thankful that you have
allowed me to be part of your life in such a meaningful way.

Adonica, our journey together has been filled with laughter, lessons, encouragement, and unspoken understanding. You
have left an indelible mark on my life, shaping me through your
friendship, your wisdom, and your unwavering faith in who I
could become. For all of this — and for simply being you — I am
endlessly grateful.

**To my godsister, Nicole Bolden, and my goddaughter, Amber
House** — your presence in my life is one of the most precious
gifts I've been given. You both represent love in its purest form —
love that uplifts, love that endures, and love that expects nothing
in return.

Nicole, your loyalty, compassion, and wisdom have been a constant source of strength and reassurance. You have a rare ability to understand without judgment, to encourage without pretense, and to love with an authenticity that brings peace to my soul. You have stood beside me through laughter and through tears, offering words that heal and a presence that calms. Your friendship is not just a bond — it is a sisterhood, a covenant of the heart that I treasure deeply.

Amber, your light shines with a joy that is contagious. You move through life with a spirit so vibrant and pure that it brightens every space you enter. Your laughter brings warmth, your kindness brings hope, and your faith reminds me that God's goodness continues through generations. Watching you grow and blossom fills me with pride and gratitude — you are a reflection of love, legacy, and limitless potential.

Together, the two of you embody the true beauty of chosen family — those who are connected not by blood, but by divine purpose. You remind me that family is built from hearts that choose one another again and again, through every season of life.

I am profoundly thankful for both of you — for the laughter we share, the prayers we've whispered, and the strength we've drawn from one another. Nicole and Amber, you are blessings beyond measure, and I thank God for weaving our lives together in such a powerful and meaningful way.

My Circle of Strength

There is a sacred circle of people in my life whom I can call at a moment's notice — whether for an encouraging word, a heartfelt conversation, or a powerful prayer when I need it most. This role you each play in my life will never be taken for granted, because your presence, your faith, and your love mean more to me than words could ever fully express.

Gwendolyn Hutchison (my brother's wife), Pastor Valorie Holcomb, Elder Dana Holcomb, Elder Roderick and Lisa Smith, Brittni Berry, Jamie Perinne, Nicole West, Wade Smart, Stephen Chapital, Melody Colebrook, Temeka Jennings, Dedra Brown, Travis Spencer, Garnett Givans, Tiffany Tibbs, Trimeka Tibbs, Clita Walker, Eloyce Walker, Evelyn Munson, and Carolyn Munson — you are each an essential part of my journey. You have touched this book and my life in ways far deeper than you may ever know. Through your wisdom, prayers, encouragement, and unwavering love, you have helped carry me through seasons of growth, challenge, and transformation.

Each of you has been a light in moments of darkness, a steady voice of reason when my path felt uncertain, and a reflection of God's goodness in human form. Your friendship is a covering of grace — one that strengthens my spirit and reminds me daily that I am never alone in this walk.

If by chance I have overlooked anyone who has lifted me, prayed for me, or spoken life into me, please know this comes not from forgetfulness of the heart, but from the limits of memory. **Charge it to my head, and not my heart.**

This acknowledgment is more than gratitude — it is a declaration of how deeply you are valued. You are my circle of strength, my family in faith, and my reminder that love, when shared freely, can sustain the soul.

From the depths of my heart — **thank you.**

ABOUT THE AUTHOR

Born in Baton Rouge, Louisiana, and raised in Oakland, California, E.J. Hutchison grew up between two worlds — one rooted in southern warmth and tradition, the other alive with rhythm, resilience, and the lessons of perseverance. His journey has been one of transformation, of finding light through loss and clarity through faith.

Writing, for him, has never been just about words. It's been a way of listening — to God, to his own heart, and to the quiet truths that often go unnoticed in the rush of life. Through every page, he strives to share the moments that shaped him, the prayers that carried him, and the grace that continues to unfold along the way.

His work is deeply personal, spiritual, and transparent — born out of a desire to remind others that they are never forgotten, never unseen, and never beyond the reach of God's love. He writes for those who have and currently walked through storms, who have doubted their strength, as well as who are still searching for meaning in the spaces between pain and peace.

Now living in The Washington, D.C., area, he continues to write from a place of reflection and gratitude, often in the quiet company of his loyal Doberman, Onyx. For eight years, Onyx has been more than a companion — he's been a silent witness to every late-night writing session, every tear, and every answered prayer.

Through his writing, E.J. Hutchison hopes to remind readers that every chapter of life — even the difficult ones — serves a divine purpose. His message is simple but enduring: that God restores, redeems, and renews all things in His time.